What are ministers saying about Daniel King's book "Healing Power?"

I loved this book and I think you will, too.
Marilyn Hickey - *Marilyn Hickey Ministries*

This is one of the best books I have ever read on the subject of healing. When I host a School of Healing, Daniel King is the first person I call.
Mike Murdock - *The Wisdom Center*

Daniel King is doing the ministry of healing. He is full of Jesus and passionate to share God's love everywhere. This book will help build your faith in God's Healing Power.
Billy Joe Daugherty - *Victory Christian Center*

"Healing Power" will prove to be an important tool in this end time global harvest. Daniel King has not only clearly presented healing truths, but he has demonstrated them in his own life and ministry. Get ready for a miracle as you read this powerful book!
Dr. Mike Francen - *Francen World Outreach*

Daniel King represents a new generation of missionary/ evangelists which are radically committed to serving God and his purposes in the earth. Daniel brings a tremendous family spiritual heritage to his ministry, where integrity and faithfulness are the norm. His latest book "Healing Power" will raise your intimacy with God, put greater faith in your heart, and motivate you to pray for hurting people like never before.
Billy Allen - *Christ for the Nations Church*

Daniel King is a mighty man of valor. God is using him to bring healing to the sick, and his book, "Healing Power" is just the antidote the sick need to receive God's healing power.

Tom Brown - *Word of Life*

I bought your book...and wooooooowwwwww what an anointed, amazing book...it changed my life.

Pastor Leon Kotze *in South Africa*

The main idea of *Healing Power* is that healing is neither exclusive nor not-of-reach. Its not something that happens to only very spiritual people. It is the heritage of every child of God...

Dagunduro Oluwafemi *in Africa*

I found Daniel King's book "Healing Power" to be very insightful... it contains a lot of relevant information.

Tim Hawryluk *in Canada*

Daniel King's teaching is very simple but profound so everyone can understand it and act upon it. He preaches the word of faith with great boldness. We are very pleased with his ministry.

Chuck Kennedy - *Faith International Christian Center*

Healing Power

Experiencing the Miracle Touch of Jesus!

Daniel King

Healing Power: Experiencing the Miracle Touch of Jesus
ISBN 978-0615787145

Copyright 2003 by:
Daniel King
King Ministries International
PO Box 701113
Tulsa, OK 74170
1-877-431-4276
www.kingministries.com

Table of Contents

Forward
by Marilyn Hickey

As the chairperson of Oral Roberts University Board of Regents, I have time and again, seen God dramatically use the students and alumni of ORU all around the world - especially in healings and miracles. Through the heritage of its founder, ORU continues to bring divine healing to our world.

Healing isn't the exclusive realm of people in ministry or a few specially gifted men and woman who become houshold names. It doesn't require super faith, even mustard-seed belief will bring your miracle. Healing isn't a spiritual feeling, it is a fact, and like any spiritual truth, it is available to everyone. Every Christain has healing in their hands - *to be healed* or to bring healing to others!

Daniel King, a recent alumnus of ORU, has taken the truth about healing and put it in a very exciting book. It will cause your faith for miracles to leap within you. I loved this book and I think you will, too. I'm sure it will release God's "healing power" into *your* life.

Letter to the Reader

This book has only one purpose. It is designed to get people healed. Revealed within these pages are the secrets to God's healing power.

My goal is to build your faith for healing. If you are sick, I want you to use the truths found inside this book to get well. If you know someone who is sick, I want you to give this book to him or her. If you hunger for manifestations of healing in your personal life, I want you to learn how to flow in the supernatural.

There are several features used to accomplish these goals in this book. They include:

Secrets of Healing Power: God has given the church many tools for healing. I carefully explain how to use each of these tools in order to be healed.

Healing Stories: Some of the most important healing stories of the Bible are retold. At the end of each account are "Power Points" which explain key healing concepts illustrated by the story.

Questions and Answers: The most frequently asked questions about healing are answered.

Bonus Section: 6,000 years of healing history.

After you finish reading this book, I believe your faith for healing will skyrocket. I look forward to hearing your healing testimony.

Taking healing power around the world,

Daniel King

Introduction

Why do I believe in healing? I was only ten years old when I first saw God's healing power at work. The boy was about my age and he was completely deaf and mute. With the trusting faith of a child I prayed for him, believing God would heal him, and God did!

It was the first night I ever spent outside the United States. My parents were traveling evangelists and our family had a two-week break between crusades, so we decided to go on a mission trip into Mexico.

It was quite the experience. Our tiny blue Toyota was stuffed full with the family and all the suitcases. None of us kids had ever been outside of the country before so we were both excited and naive. Right after we crossed the border, I remember being disappointed because none of the Mexicans I could see were wearing big hats and ponchos.

We knew absolutely no Spanish so my dad pulled out a Spanish-English Dictionary and began to teach us words like "por favor" and "gracias." Those few hours of language training were all I had to prepare me to be thrown into a world where everyone spoke a foreign language.

Back in those days the Mexican roads were primitive. They were bumpy, dusty, and narrow. After a full day of driving, we arrived at a tiny village in the middle of nowhere. Some friends had given us directions and a letter of introduction addressed to a pastor in this small settlement.

We found the house and knocked on the door. The pastor, who looked at least seventy years of age, answered the door. My father handed him the letter of introduction. The pastor read it and invited us in.

The man motioned for our family to sit down at the kitchen table, and he immediately began feeding us. As we ate, people from the village stopped by to see who the strange visitors were. After taking one look at us, they raced off to their homes and came running back with hands full of food as well as a train of family members behind them eager to see the strange sight. In a few minutes the entire kitchen was full of people who had contributed to the feast.

After we finished eating, the pastor asked my dad to preach. This was a dilemma. None of the villagers knew a word of English, and we hardly spoke any of their language. How in the world does one go about preaching to Spanish speakers if one does not know a lick of Spanish?

Well, my father hit upon a brilliant idea. He opened his Bible and began reading verses in English. He pointed to a scripture and one of the young ladies who could read found the same verse in her Spanish Bible. She read it to the crowd who was packed into the house.

The subject of the message was healing. My dad pointed to Psalm 103:3 and the girl read it in Spanish, God *"forgives all your sins and heals all your diseases."* Then he found 1 Peter 2:24, *"by his wounds you have been healed."* Finally, he read several stories about Jesus healing the sick. By the time the sermon was finished, we had gone through almost every healing scripture in God's Word. After that, our family started to pray for the sick.

A young boy, who appeared to be the same age as me, was pushed forward. Since he was my height, I laid my hands on him. When I finished praying, he began to make really weird sounds with his mouth. When the people heard the sounds he was making, everyone erupted with excitement. They began dancing and praising God. Shouts of "Hallelujah" filled the room.

Our family did not really know what was going on, but we joined in the celebration. It was not until two weeks later, when we arrived back in the United States, that we discovered the full extent of the miracle. We were telling the story to the people who had originally given us the letter of introduction, and they got excited. They eagerly asked us questions. Was it a little brown haired boy? What kind of sounds did he make? What was the reaction of the crowd? Then they told us that the little boy was born deaf and mute. He had never made a sound before in his life. So, that night God had opened up his ears and loosened his tongue, and he had made noise for the first time in his life!

God used me as a ten-year-old to bring his healing power to a little boy who desperately needed God's touch. What an experience! Since then, I have witnessed thousands of miracles. I have seen blind eyes open, lame people walk, chronic headaches gone, cancer vanish, horrible skin diseases clear up, deaf ears hear, and tumors disappear. All these miracles have absolutely convinced me that God's healing touch is available to every single person who needs it! All you need to do is use your faith to reach out and touch God.

You can be healed!

How can you know God will heal you?

I have a beautiful cousin who just turned four years old. She is a bundle of joy, energy, and enthusiasm, but she is a handful when I play with her. Since she tires me out after ten minutes, I am not sure how her parents keep up with her.

One day I was watching her and she told me she wanted some snacks. I told her she needed to wait until dinnertime, but she did not agree with me.

"I want a snack."

"No, you need to wait until later."

"Daniel, I want a snack now."

"You will spoil your appetite for dinner."

"I want a snack!"

"No"

"Yes"

"No"

After arguing with her for a minute, I asked her, "Rachel, why are you so determined to have a snack?"

With impeccable four-year-old logic, she explained, "Because my daddy says I can." After that, I was forced to give in to her demands. I gave her a snack.

It did not really matter what I told her, all that mattered in her mind was what her daddy had said. As far as she was concerned, my words were meaningless. Her daddy said she could have a snack, and she was not going to quit until she received a snack. In the same way, it does not really matter what people around you are saying about your healing; all that matters is what your Heavenly Daddy says.

"Why are you going to be healed?"

"Because my Daddy says I am going to be healed."

If an earthly father will give good gifts to his children, how much more will your Father in heaven give good gifts to those who ask him? (Matthew 7:11).

God wants to heal you!

"How do you know healing is for today?" a man asked me recently.

"I know healing is for today because God does not change," I replied.

Every day the world changes. (Change is an inevitable part of life: circumstances change, people change their minds, governments change their laws, and businesses change their locations.) In the midst of all this world's hustle and bustle, there is only one person who does not change. God does not change. He declares, *"I the LORD do not change"* (Malachi 3:6). If God healed the sick in the past, He will heal the sick today.

Jesus, like His Father, does not change either. *"Jesus Christ is the same yesterday and today and forever"* (Hebrews 13:8). Since Jesus healed the blind, the cripples, the lepers, and the paralyzed when He walked on earth; He still heals the sick today.

Unfortunately, some in the church have changed God's "I am the Lord who heals you" to "I was the Lord who healed you." These people acknowledge that God healed in the past, but they refuse to believe that He heals today. I want you to know that God's healing power is not past tense, it is present tense.

James writes, *"Don't be deceived, my dear brothers. Every good and perfect gift* [including healing] *is from above, coming down from the Father of the heavenly lights, who does not change like shifting shadows"* (James 1:16-17). On a dark night shadows change as the moonrises but God is not like those ever-changing shadows, He does not change over time.

Healing is a good gift that comes from God. In this book you can read stories about God healing during Old Testament times, Jesus healing when He was on earth, the Apostles healing during the early days of the church, believers healing throughout church history, and healings which I have seen with my own eyes. God does not change. If He has healed all these people over thousands of years, He is absolutely willing to heal you right now.

I also know healing is for today because God does not lie. *"God is not a man, that he should lie, nor a son of man, that he should change his mind. Does he speak and then not act? Does he promise and not fulfill?"* (Numbers 23:19). The Bible is filled with promises of healing, and if God promised healing, He will be faithful to keep His word.

Healing is for you today. This is your day for a miracle!

Expect a miracle touch

Receiving from God is like being the receiver in a football game. When the quarterback throws the ball, the receiver must reach up and catch it from the air. No matter how great the quarterback can throw, if the receiver just stands there, the ball is going to bounce off his head. God has thrown a beautiful healing pass right at you, reach your hands up into the air and receive it from Him right now. Do not let the enemy cornerback snatch the ball from within your grasp. Reach up, claim what is rightfully yours and run with it into the end zone for a Holy Spirit touchdown!

The world is full of sickness, but while Christians might live in the world, we do not belong to the world (John 15:19). Our citizenship is in heaven where there is no pain and no disease. The blessings of heaven do not have to wait for the future; you can enjoy heaven's benefits right now while you are still in this world. God wants His *"will to be done on earth as it is in heaven"* (Matthew 6:10). You can overcome sickness because the one who is in you is greater than the one who is in the world (1 John 4:4).

Jesus Christ is the same yesterday, today, and forever! His touch is just as real today as when He touched the blind man's eyes, reached out towards the leper, or stroked the hand of the feverous woman. Stop reading for a second and imagine the hand of Jesus touching you softly on your forehead. One touch from His hand has healed thousands and one touch can heal you.

Remember, Jesus was never sick a day of His life, and we should be just like Him.

Healing is at the heart of Jesus' ministry

When Jesus lived on earth, He had a three-fold ministry composed of preaching, teaching, and healing. All three were essential components of Jesus' ministry. Preaching ministers to the spirit, teaching feeds the soul (the mind, will, and emotions), and healing provides for the body.

Preaching announces the existence of the power of God, teaching explains the nature of the power of God, and miracles are manifestations of the power of God. Healing miracles serve as proof that the message of Jesus is true.

The three-part ministry of Jesus could be compared to the three dimensions of a room. A room has height, depth, and width. If any one of these three dimensions are removed, one is left with nothing. In the same way, if preaching is removed from ministry, it is difficult to win anyone to Christ. If teaching is removed from ministry, one's mind will not understand the ways of God. If healing and miracles are removed, then one is left with a powerless God. All three are indispensable for a complete Christian life.

Divine healing was an essential part of Jesus' ministry, because it validated His message. Without healing, the words of Jesus are nothing more than moral teachings. With healing, the words of Jesus are proven to be the words of God Himself.

Thomas Jefferson, one of America's founding fathers, did not believe in supernatural healing. He wrote his own version of the Gospels where he took out all the stories about Jesus healing people. However, his powerless rendition of the life of Jesus is barely remembered today because the ethical teachings of Jesus without the miracles of Jesus are nothing but powerless religious guidelines.

Visible healings demonstrate the miracle of the Incarnation. When Jesus was born as a baby, God became man. By cloaking Himself with a thin covering of skin, He assumed the pains and joys of His creation. This stupendous event marked the explosion of the kingdom of heaven upon an unsuspecting world.

Healing was an important part of Jesus' ministry because He wanted people to be whole: spirit, mind, and body. Healing is just as important to Jesus today as it was when He walked on earth. Healing is available for you right now.

Get ready for your healing

Faith is built as God's Word becomes real in our lives. This book is full of scripture. All the chapters I have written have one thing in common; they will ignite your faith for healing. You do not have to read them in order. Feel free to skip around. But, I encourage you to ask God to increase your faith as you read each chapter.

I have identified sixteen ways for you to be healed. Why does God have so many ways? It is because God will use any method He can to get healing to His children. In this book I have included as much information as possible on each way God chooses to heal.

Get ready, your healing shall quickly appear!

The Healing Power
of The Anointing

T he anointing is the manifest presence of God's power and it releases healing power. The first time Jesus taught in His hometown of Nazareth, He read from the book of Isaiah. This was His text on that momentous occasion, *"The Spirit of the Lord is on me, because he has anointed me..."* Jesus was anointed by the Holy Spirit.

Why was this anointing important? In the ancient kingdom of Israel, prophets poured a bottle of anointing oil (which represented the Holy Spirit) over the head of the one God chose for a special task. For example, a man called to be king was specifically anointed for the job of being king.

Well, Jesus was anointed for a special task. Let's read the rest of the text Jesus read, *"The Spirit of the Lord is on me, because he has anointed me to preach good news to the poor. He has sent me to proclaim freedom for the prisoners and recovery of sight for the blind, to release the oppressed, to proclaim the year of the Lord's favor"* (Luke 4:18-19). Jesus was anointed to preach good news, to proclaim freedom to those who were held in the bondage of sickness, to heal the blind, and to set free those who suffered under the oppression of Satan. In short, Jesus was anointed to bring healing.

Some people think the word "Christ" is nothing but Jesus' last name, but in reality this word "Christ" is a title that means "Anointed One." The anointing was so important in the life of

From Tragedy to Triumph

A woman in Honduras shared her tragic story with us. She was sitting in a wheelchair to the right side of the platform. She revealed, "One night eleven years ago, my husband came home drunk and angry. He started to beat me with his fists. He beat me so severely that for eleven years I have been unable to walk."

As I preached about how Jesus heals the sick, God began to strengthen the woman's legs. With a great act of faith, she pushed herself up out of the wheelchair. For a few seconds she wobbled, but then she took a small step and another step. Within a few minutes she came running up on the platform shouting, "Jesus healed me! Jesus healed me!"

Jesus that everyone who knew Him called Him "Jesus - the Anointed One."

Did Jesus use His anointing to bring healing? In Acts 10:38, we discover that *"...God anointed Jesus of Nazareth with the Holy Ghost and with power: [he] went about doing good, and healing all that were oppressed of the devil; for God was with him"* (KJV).

The word "oppressed" used in this verse is a compound Greek word formed from the preposition *kata* meaning, "down or under," and *dunasteuo* meaning, "I hold power or lordship." So this word refers to those who are held down under the power of Satan. You can understand the full meaning of the word if you will imagine a slave master using a whip to force a slave to carry a heavy burden. The slave is held down by the oppression of the master.

Sickness is a cruel taskmaster which oppresses and enslaves. Jesus came to set us free from the slavery of sin and disease. Jesus is anointed to release us from the burden of sickness.

The anointing destroys the yoke of sickness

"And it shall come to pass in that day, that his burden shall be taken away from off thy shoulder, and his yoke from off thy neck, and the yoke shall be destroyed because of the anointing" (Isaiah 10:27 KJV).

7

During Bible times oxen were used to plow fields. A thick yoke was hung around their necks and a plow was attached to the yoke. For hours on end, the oxen would be forced to walk up and down fields dragging heavy plows through the earth. The yoke represented a great weight and a burden. Isaiah says the anointing power of God destroys the yoke. In other words, the anointing wrecks, demolishes, and ruins every weight and burden.

Sickness is a great burden. Your body may feel like it has been dragging around a great weight, but the anointing of God has the power to destroy the yoke of sickness. As we read just a moment ago, Jesus came to preach deliverance to captives (Luke 4:18). The sick are held captive by the yoke of illness, but the anointing of Jesus brings deliverance from the captivity of infirmity.

We can be anointed just as Jesus was anointed

If Jesus was already God, why would He need a special anointing to heal the sick? Jesus may have been God, but when He came to earth, He left his divine powers behind. We know this from Philippians 2:6-8, *"[Jesus], being in very nature God, did not consider equality with God something to be grasped, but made himself nothing, taking the very nature of a servant, being made in human likeness. And being found in appearance as a man, he humbled himself...."*

Since Jesus appeared on earth as a man, He was unable to do anything supernatural unless He did it through the power of the anointing. Jesus did not speak one single word under his own power, instead He only spoke the words His Father told Him to say. *"... The words I say to you are not just my own. Rather, it is the Father, living in me, who is doing his work"* (John 14:10). The miraculous works of Jesus were not done under His own human power, they were accomplished through the anointing of the Holy Spirit and the guidance of His Father.

Jesus was the Son of God, but He healed the sick as a man anointed by the Spirit of God. Every miracle of Jesus was performed

8

through the power of the anointing. Now, are you ready for some good news? Because Jesus performed all His miracles as an anointed human being, we can perform the same miracles if we are anointed. We can be anointed in the same way Jesus was. He promised, *"Very truly, I tell you, the one who believes in me will also do the works that I do and, in fact, will do greater works than these, because I am going to the Father"* (John 14:12 NRSV). If we are anointed with the same Spirit as Jesus, we can do the same works He did, and even greater works.

When Jesus commissioned the twelve disciples, he assigned them the same mission that He had been sent to accomplish. In Matthew 10:1, Jesus gives the disciples authority to heal *"every disease and sickness."* In Luke 10:9, Jesus commands the seventy to heal the sick. Again, in Mark 16:18, believers are told that if they place their hands on sick people, they will get well. In all three cases, the followers of Jesus are commanded to do the same works Jesus did. The disciples were instructed to preach the exact same message Jesus preached and were anointed to perform precisely the same miracles He did. Since the authority given to the disciples extends across the centuries and now rests in the hands of every believer, today's church can expect the same miracles. Healing should be a normal part of every Christian's life.

Why do you think we are called Christians? Remember, I told you the word "Christ" means "Anointed One." This means the word "Christian" can be translated as "little anointed one." As Christians we are anointed just as Jesus was anointed!

Three Facts About the Anointing

1. The anointing is measurable

Elisha asked for a double-portion of Elijah's anointing, and he received it (2 Kings 2:9). We know Elisha received double the anointing because the Bible records twice as many miracles that he performed than Elijah did during his lifetime.

Jesus had the anointing without measure (John 3:34). Any one human being only has a measured amount of the anointing because if we had the anointing without measure, our human bodies would not be able to handle the overwhelming power. Jesus flowed in all the gifts of the Spirit and He was anointed for every ministry office.

Today God anoints Christian leaders for a specific ministry office. Some are anointed to be pastors, some prophets, some evangelists, some teachers, some to help others, and some to be administrators (Ephesians 4:11; 1 Corinthians 12:28), but only Jesus was anointed with the fullness of all the ministry gifts and callings.

2. The anointing is transferable
When the woman with the issue of blood touched the hem of Christ's garment, she instantly felt a transfer of healing power into her body (Mark 5:25-34). On another occasion, healing power was again conveyed by a piece of cloth that had become saturated with the anointing. This happened when the Apostle Paul laid his hands on cloth handkerchiefs and those pieces of fabric were used to heal the sick. The anointing was transferred from the hands of Paul into the cloth and then carried to those who desperately needed help (Acts 19:12).

The church at Antioch laid hands on Paul and Barnabas and the anointing was transferred to their lives (Acts 13:3). Later, as Paul laid hands on Timothy the gift of God (anointing) was transferred to Timothy's life (2 Timothy 1:6). From these examples, we see that the anointing is transferable.

3. The anointing is tangible
The power of God can be felt by the physical body. Jesus felt anointing power leave his body when the woman with the issue of blood touched him and she felt power enter her body as she was

healed. The anointing is not a figment of the imagination; it can be touched and experienced. Many times I have felt the power of God in my hands when I am praying for people. I can actually feel the anointing leave my body and flow into another person. On other occasions, I have felt the anointing as bolts of electricity shooting through an entire room. Often one can feel the presence of God hovering in a room like a cloud right above the heads of the audience.

The Healing Power
of The Compassion of Jesus

My brother and I were on our way to an important meeting when we saw an old man standing by the side of the road hitchhiking. He was dressed in an old, thread-worn suit but it looked nicely pressed. We commented that someone should stop and give the man a ride. Then an idea hit us, we should take compassion on him and lend him a helping hand. At the next exit, we turned around and went back to where the man was standing with his thumb outstretched.

When he was safely in our car, he told us he had been standing out in the freezing wind for forty-five minutes. Hundreds of cars had passed him, but no one stopped to help. A group of teenagers had even slowed down and thrown beer bottles at him. He was in a city that has some of the greatest churches in the world, yet no one had time to help him.

Why did we stop to help the man? Because we had compassion on him. Other people may have felt pity for the man, but their pity did not compel them to stop. We helped him, because we had compassion.

In mystery stories detectives look for the motives of criminals who commit crimes. If Jesus was on trial for healing the sick, compassion would be His motive. One of the main reasons Jesus helped people was because He was filled with compassion.

The healing ministry of Jesus flowed from His compassion. One day, when Jesus left His boat, He was greeted by a large crowd, and *"he had compassion on them and healed their sick"* (Matthew 14:14). When two blind men cried out to Jesus, He *"had compassion on them and touched their eyes. Immediately they received their sight"* (Matthew 20:34). A leper got down on his knees and begged Jesus to heal him, *"filled with compassion, Jesus reached out his hand and touched the man. 'I am willing,' he said. 'Be clean!'"* (Mark 1:41).

On numerous occasions, Jesus was moved with compassion. The Greek word for "compassion" is *splanchnos* which refers to a deep inner feeling. Have you ever experienced such a strong emotion that you felt it in the deepest pit of your stomach? This word is the strongest expression of compassion in the Greek language and it is used many times by the Gospel writers to explain Christ's motivation for healing the sick.

Jesus did not just feel sorry for people, He fixed their problems. Sympathy makes us want to sit down and have a pity party with the hurting person. Compassion, on the other hand, makes us want to do something to fix the problem.

Where did the compassion of Jesus come from? The answer is found in Psalm 116:5, *"our God is full of compassion."* Jesus was filled with compassion because His Father was compassionate. In His private prayer times, Jesus adopted the compassionate attitude of His Father for the sick. Healing is a visible representation of God's innermost feelings of love for humankind. Jesus healed the man at the pool of Bethesda (John 5:1-15) out of His compassion, not in response to the man's faith. This explains why many non-Christians are healed, God simply has compassion for hurting people. He heals people because of His overwhelming love.

PRESCRIPTION FOR HEALTH

"'I will restore you to health and
heal your wounds,' declares
the LORD"
(Jeremiah 30:17)

Dr. Jesus

The Healing Power
of Faith

" *Have faith in God," Jesus answered. "I tell you the truth, if anyone says to this mountain, 'Go, throw yourself into the sea,' and does not doubt in his heart but believes that what he says will happen, it will be done for him. Therefore I tell you, whatever you ask for in prayer, believe that you have received it, and it will be yours"* (Mark 11:22-24).

According to this verse, you can have anything you ask for in prayer if you have enough faith. Does "anything" include healing? Absolutely! James says, *"the prayer offered in faith will make the sick person well"* (James 5:15). Faith plays a vital role in the healing process.

What is faith?

Faith is trusting God when there is no one else to trust. Faith is relying upon God in the midst of trouble. Faith is having confidence in God's promises. Faith sees the invisible and believes the impossible. Faith is a conviction that no matter what the circumstances look like, God will fulfill His word. Faith is knowing beyond a shadow of a doubt that God will heal you. Faith is believing in God more than you believe in your sickness.

I agree with Oral Roberts, "There are no bonds faith cannot break, no fetters it cannot sever, no dungeon it cannot open, no disease it cannot heal, no victory it cannot win." F.F. Bosworth said,

"Faith does not wait for the walls to fall down; faith shouts them down." T.L. Osborn explained, "Faith is believing that God will do what you know He said in His word that He would do....There are just two platforms on which to stand: One is belief; the other, unbelief. Either the word of God is true, or it is not. God will either do what He has promised, or He will not. His promises are either reliable, or they are not." Faith in God is a black and white issue, there is no gray area involved in trusting God's promises.

According to Hebrews 11:1, *"Now faith is the substance of things hoped for, the evidence of things not seen"* (KJV). Have you ever read a detective story? By carefully examining a crime scene, a sleuth reconstructs what happened during a crime. Tiny clues provide evidence of events not seen. Faith is the same; it provides absolute proof of things we cannot see. Bosworth said, "It is not, as many unthinking persons suppose, believing without evidence, but believing because of the highest possible evidence, God's Word...."

Valentino and His Father

In the nation of the Dominican Republic, an argument brewed in one home. "I don't believe in God," Valentino's father declared, "My son is not going to the healing festival." His wife begged and pleaded, "Please, let us go to the meeting. Our son is deaf and dumb. Perhaps a miracle will happen."

"Absolutely not! If there is no God, then there are no miracles either. Valentino is not going tonight."

However, in direct disobedience, Valentino's mother and grandmother snuck him out of the house and brought him to the meeting. One of the team members prayed for Valentino and to everyone's delight God opened his ears and the eight-year-old boy began to speak for the first time. They brought him to the platform and I whispered in Valentino's ear, "Hallelujah." The boy repeated the word. The crowd went wild.

Arriving home that night, Valentino greeted his father with a huge smile saying "Papa" for the first time. With tears in his eyes, the tough cynical man who refused to believe in God, fell to his knees and gave his life to Jesus.

Recently I purchased a plane ticket. When I bought the ticket, I did not demand to see the plane I would be riding in. I had faith the plane would be at the airport when the time arrived for me to leave on my trip. The ticket represented the promise of the airline. Faith is like that ticket; it is the substance that guarantees God's promises will come true. Faith is your ticket to healing.

We should *"live by faith, not by sight"* (2 Corinthians 5:7). Faith is similar to the title deed to a property you have never seen. Once the title of a property belongs to you, the property also belongs to you. You can say with assurance, "I own this land" even though you have never seen it.

Bosworth believes faith could be called a "sixth sense." By using faith, we sense things in the spiritual realm. When we sense something by faith, we do not need to experience it with our other senses to know it is real. This truth can be demonstrated when you think about how we use our other senses. When you see a building off in the distance, you do not doubt its existence until you are close enough to touch it or taste it. No, you believe the building is there even when only one sense confirms that it is real. In the same way, if your "faith sense" informs you of your healing, you do not need to wait until your other senses catch up to know the truth of your healing. Eventually, you will be able to touch, taste, see, hear, and smell what your faith sense has been telling you all along.

Where does faith come from?

Jesus is both the *"author and the finisher"* of our faith (Hebrews 12:2 KJV). Jesus is the source of our faith, He is the object of our faith, and He is the one who guarantees our faith.

The Apostle Paul wrote, *"faith comes from hearing the message, and the message is heard through the word of Christ"* (Romans 10:17). In the Gospels, faith came to the sick as they listened to the preaching of Jesus and as they watched Him healing illnesses. As Jesus healed the sick, *"News about him spread"* (Matthew 4:24).

When the multitudes heard reports about Jesus' healing ability, faith was ignited in their hearts to believe for their own healing. Faith is ignited when we hear the Word of God. The hearing comes before the healing. Listening to faith-filled preaching produces faith and faith produces healing. As we hear reports of Jesus' healing ability, faith grows in our hearts to believe for healing. God has already given a measure of faith to every person (Romans 12:3), but the more we hear God's Word, the greater our faith grows.

Paul preached the *"word of faith"* (Romans 10:8), and as a result saw many miracles in his ministry. As he taught, his words created faith in his listeners, which enabled Paul to demonstrate the gospel with the Spirit's power (1 Corinthians 2:4).

Faith is essential for a healing miracle

We absolutely need faith. Repeatedly, the Bible drives this point home with this simple verse, *"The righteous shall live by faith"* (Habakkuk 2:4; Romans 1:17; Galatians 3:11; Hebrews 10:38). Those in right standing before God must live by faith. You will live or die based on your level of faith in God. Because *"...without faith it is impossible to please God...anyone who comes to him must believe that he exists and that he rewards those who earnestly seek him"* (Hebrews 11:6).

God always moves in response to faith. God is no respecter of persons, He is a respecter of faith. The Centurion told Jesus, "Just say the word and my servant will be healed." Sure enough, Jesus met him at the point of his faith when he said, "It will be done just as you believed it would." The man's servant was healed that very hour. The ruler of the synagogue asked Jesus to lay hands on his daughter, and the moment Jesus touched the girl, she was raised from the dead. Just as Jesus responded to the faith of these desperate people, the power of God will meet you at the point of your faith.

Faith is the main ingredient of a healing miracle. Releasing your faith releases healing power into the organs of your body. As soon as you release your faith, God releases a miracle.

God will move heaven and earth because of faith. Smith Wigglesworth said, "There's something about believing God that'll cause God to pass over a million people just to get to you." Faith will cause God to move on your behalf.

There are two types of people: those who say, "I'll believe it when I see it," and those who know the truth that they will see it as soon as they believe it.

Faith and power go together like a hand and a glove. God's power is the glove and faith is the hand which activates the glove. The power is inactive until the faith is present.

If you do not work your faith, your faith will not work

Faith is like a muscle, the more you use it, the greater it grows. Faith is not faith until you take action. *"Faith by itself, if it is not accompanied by action, is dead"* (James 2:17). Faith without works is dead. "Workless faith" is an oxymoron. As a matter of fact, faith without works can not even be called faith. When the four men lowered their friend through the roof, Luke says Jesus "saw their faith." In other words, he noticed a physical action that demonstrated their faith. They acted on their faith, and Jesus took notice (Luke 5:17-26).

It is vital to act on your faith. The bleeding woman acted on her faith when she desperately pushed through the crowd and touched the hem of Jesus' garment. The blind man acted on his faith when he moved towards Jesus. You put your faith in action by moving your body in a way you could not move it before. If you have a paralyzed arm, try moving it. If you could not walk, stand up and begin walking. If you have a tumor on your body, place your hand on the tumor and begin praying. Act on your faith right now by reaching out towards Jesus.

I encourage you to speak words of faith, trust in faith, act by faith, live by faith, and move by faith. Your faith is the key to your healing!

Four Levels of Faith

1. Great faith (Matthew 8:5-13)
Jesus was entering the city of Capernaum, when He saw one of the most hated men in the city walking towards Him. From a Jewish perspective, the man had three strikes against his character. First, he was a Gentile; second, he was a soldier; and third, not only was he a soldier, he was a commander in the Roman army. He was not the type of person most Jews would want to be seen with, yet Jesus stopped to talk to him.

The centurion asked Jesus for help, "Lord, I have a servant in my house who is paralyzed and in great suffering."

Out of his compassion Jesus said, "I will go and heal him."

Then the soldier said something that astounded Jesus, "Lord, I do not deserve to have you come under my roof. But just say the word, and my servant will be healed. For I myself am a man under authority, with soldiers under me. I tell this one, 'Go,' and he goes; and that one, 'Come,' and he comes. I say to my servant, 'Do this,' and he does it."

The centurion was a man who walked in great authority and he recognized the authority of Jesus. He was able to send his soldiers on errands simply by whispering a single word, and he had a tremendous faith in the ability of Jesus to heal disease by speaking a single word.

When Jesus heard this, He was amazed and said to those around him, "I tell you the truth, I have not found anyone in Israel with such great faith." In the original Greek of the story of the Canaanite woman (Matthew 15:28), Jesus calls this type of faith *"mega faith."* The centurion had "mega faith," enormous faith, gigantic faith, outstanding faith, king-sized faith. His faith was bigger than the faith of every Israelite Jesus had ever met.

Jesus was so impressed with the great faith that He said to the centurion, "Go! It will be done just as you believed it would." The moment Jesus said the word, the servant was completely healed!

2. Normal faith (Matthew 9:27-30)

Right after Jesus raised the daughter of Jairus from the dead, two blind men followed Him. In their desperation, they cried out, "Have mercy on us, Son of David!"

Jesus asked them, "Do you believe that I am able to do this?"

"Yes, Lord," the blind men replied.

Jesus touched their eyes and said, "According to your faith will it be done to you." As they heard His words, faith sprang up within their hearts, and their sight was restored. These two men heard reports of Jesus' healing power. As they heard the testimonies of others who were healed, faith was birthed inside them. Jesus met them at the point of their faith and they were healed.

3. Little faith (Matthew 8:23-27)

After a long day of preaching and healing, Jesus got in a boat and His disciples followed Him. The disciples quietly rowed as they reflected on the busy day. Suddenly, without warning, a wild storm appeared. Rain fell, the wind blew, and the waves began sweeping over the side of the boat, filling it with water.

Scared, the disciples looked at Jesus for help. To their surprise, Jesus was sleeping. The disciples debated about what they should do, but when another wave splashed into the boat they got scared. One of the disciples began shaking Jesus. When Jesus opened His eyes, they yelled, "Lord, save us! We're going to drown!"

Jesus saw the fear in their eyes and said, "You of little faith, why are you so afraid?" Then He got up and rebuked the winds and the waves, and instantly the sea was completely calm.

Jesus used the word "little" to describe the disciples' faith in this situation. This word can mean little, tiny, microscopic, and small. Jesus was disappointed in their lack of faith. Despite His hours of teaching concerning faith and despite the hundreds of miracles the disciples had seen, they still lacked a simple trust in God's protection. The faith of the disciples was replaced by fear, which is the exact opposite of faith. They were more focused on the wind and the waves than they were on God's power. They had little faith because they allowed fear to dominate their thoughts. When fear comes in, faith goes out. Great fear equals little faith. Where there is faith, there is no fear and where there is fear, there is no faith.

I believe that any action not based on faith is a sin. Maintain your faith by keeping your eyes on Jesus. Do not look at the wind and the waves of life; instead, look to your Lord.

Fear will destroy your faith by whispering lies to you. It says, "You are going to die from your sickness. You'll never get well. God is not interested in healing you." Jesus neutralized the disciples' fear by rebuking the wind and the waves. We can destroy fear by rebuking it and quoting God's Word.

Next time fear attacks you, quote these scriptures,

* *"For God hath not given us the spirit of fear; but of power, and of love, and of a sound mind"* (2 Timothy 1:7 - KJV).
* *"Surely he will save you...from the deadly pestilence. He will cover you with his feathers, and under his wings you will find refuge; his faithfulness will be your shield and rampart"* (Psalm 91:3-4).

On another occasion the disciples were trying to heal a boy who had seizures. Because of the seizures, the boy would often fall into the campfire or water. When the disciples were unable to heal the boy, Jesus was forced to heal the demon-possessed boy Himself. Later the disciples asked Jesus why they were unable to heal the boy. Jesus blamed their inability to heal on their "little faith," but then He reassured them, *"...I tell you the truth, if you have faith as small as a mustard seed, you can say to this mountain, 'Move from here to there' and it will move. Nothing will be impossible for you"* (Matthew 17:20). The mustard seed is a tiny seed, yet it grows to be one of the largest garden plants. Jesus is saying that even little faith can produce great miracles.

4. No faith (Matthew 13:54-58)

Jesus wanted to minister to the people in His hometown. With fondness he remembered the many years He had lived and worked in Nazareth. These were the people He had played with as a child. He had repaired their furniture as He worked in His step-father's carpenter shop. He had talked with them, seen them at the market place, and sat with them in the synagogue. Jesus deeply cared for His friends and acquaintances so on a Sabbath morning, He asked the rabbi if he could speak.

As Jesus began teaching, the people of His hometown were amazed. One man asked another, "Where did this man get this wisdom and these miraculous powers? Isn't this the carpenter's son?" Another said, "Isn't his mother's name Mary, and aren't his brothers James, Joseph, Simon and Judas? Aren't all his sisters with us? Where then did this man get all these things?" They took offense at Him.

Jesus was disappointed. He said to them, "Only in his hometown and in his own house is a prophet without honor."

The story has a sad aftermath. Even though Jesus wanted to bless the people from His boyhood home, *"...he did not do many miracles there because of their lack of faith"* (Matthew 13:58). They had no faith to believe for miracles, because they refused to accept that Jesus was the Son of God. Mark 6:5 tells us Jesus *"could not"* do many miracles there. The original Greek literally says Jesus "was not able" to do many miracles because of their absence of faith. Their lack of faith prevented Jesus from healing them. Imagine how sorry Jesus must have felt as He left town.

The Healing Power
of The Covenant

Right after the Israelites were delivered from the country of Egypt, God made a covenant of healing with them. In this covenant of health, God assured the Israelites if they remained obedient, they would also remain healthy. What was the significance of this covenant? During Bible times, covenants were extremely important. They represented a legally binding, life-time agreement between two parties. Today the marriage covenant is the closest thing we have to the idea of a Biblical covenant. When a man and a woman are married, they pledge mutual love and support for the rest of their lives.

The Lord decreed, *"If you listen carefully to the voice of the LORD your God and do what is right in his eyes, if you pay attention to his commands and keep all his decrees, I will not bring on you any of the dis-*

"Jesus Healed My Blind Baby"

In Juba, Sudan, thousands of people were packed tightly around the platform. Suddenly, I observed a baby being passed from hand to hand over the top of the crowd. Within a few moments, the baby was placed on the stage. Not knowing why the baby was passed forward, I picked the baby up in my arms and began to rock it. The infant looked up at me and I saw bright brown eyes staring into mine. Twenty minutes later the child's mother had managed to push her way through the crowd to claim him. I asked her, "Mama, why did you send your baby to the front?" She replied, "My baby was blind in both eyes, but after the prayer for the sick, my son is able to see!"

eases I brought on the Egyptians, for I am the LORD, who heals you" (Exodus 15:26). Some Bible scholars believe this should be translated, "I will not permit on you any of the diseases I permitted on the Egyptians." The diseases that attacked the people of Egypt were not the result of God's malevolent actions, instead they were caused by Pharaoh's disobedience.

The terms of God's healing covenant were simple; obey God and you will walk in health. God promised them, *"Worship the LORD your God, and....I will take away sickness from among you"* (Exodus 23:25). God guaranteed to take away all sickness from among His children in return for their sincere worship. Later God reaffirmed His covenant, *"The LORD will keep you free from every disease"* (Deuteronomy 7:15).

We know God kept His promise because years later the Israelites were still singing songs about a miraculous time of divine health in the desert, *"...he brought his people safely out of Egypt, loaded with silver and gold; there were no sick or feeble people among them"* (Psalm 105:37 NLT). When the three million Israelites left Egypt, there were no sick or even feeble people among their number. It was a period of miraculous health. Zero disease, zero sickness, no cripples, no blind people; all the children of Abraham were healed by God's power.

Unfortunately, the Israelites did not keep their part of the covenant. They broke their promises and began to disobey God. This was a great tragedy.

All covenants have benefits if both parties keep their side of the bargain, and penalties if one of the parties breaks a promise. The covenant God made with Israel was no different. In Deuteronomy 28 we find a list of blessings for obeying God's commands. These blessings include abundant prosperity, divine health, and protection.

However, there are also penalties (called curses) for disobedience. These penalties include a depressingly long list of diseases including: fever, inflammation, wasting disease, boils, tumors, festering sores, incurable itches, madness, blindness, confusion of mind, lingering illnesses, and every kind of sickness and disease. Sickness is part of the curse for disobeying God.

Jesus reversed the curse

Jesus came to set us free from the curse! *"Christ redeemed us from the curse of the law by becoming a curse for us..."* (Galatians 3:13). Jesus died on the cross to pay the price for sin. He took the curse of sin and sickness upon His own body, and now we are set free from the curse. Jesus reversed the curse and replaced it with the blessings of Abraham for everyone who has faith (Galatians 3:14).

God originally formed His covenant with the Israelites, but through Jesus this covenant has been extended to all who believe. Paul said, *"Understand, then, that those who believe are children of Abraham"* (Galatians 3:7). This means that according to God's covenant, we can walk in divine health if we obey God.

This covenant of health is unbreakable, unshakeable, and ever-lasting. God promised, *"I will not violate my covenant or alter what my lips have uttered"* (Psalm 89:34). As long as we keep our part of the covenant by obeying God, He will keep His part of the covenant by healing us.

PRESCRIPTION FOR HEALTH

"Jesus went through all the towns and villages, teaching in their synagogues, preaching the good news of the kingdom and healing every disease and sickness."
(Matthew 9:35)

Dr. Jesus

The Healing Power of
The Atonement

Healing and salvation are closely linked. When Jesus died on the cross, He paid the price for both our salvation and our healing. The church has focused on the miracle of salvation, but salvation is only part of the priceless gift Jesus purchased with His blood. Healing is also part of the atonement.

What is the atonement? The price for sin is death; therefore, every time a person sins the penalty must be paid in blood. In the Old Testament God told the Israelites to use animal sacrifices to atone (pay for) their sins. When Jesus died on the cross He became our ultimate sacrifice, and His blood paid the price for all our sins. So, the term "atonement" refers to Christ's work on the cross that atoned for all our sins and cured all the effects of sin, including sickness.

According to Psalm 103:3, God *"...forgives all your sins and heals all your diseases."* Forgiveness and healing are inseparable. They are like two sides of the same coin. Right before Jesus healed the paralyzed man who was let down through the roof, He forgave the man's sins. In the ministry of Jesus both forgiveness and healing were essential.

This verse proves that salvation and healing are connected. *"... The prayer offered in faith will make the sick person well; the Lord will raise him up. If he has sinned, he will be forgiven"* (James 5:15). Notice the prayer of faith will heal the sick, and cause the forgiveness of sins. The same prayer produces both salvation from sins and healing from sickness!

The Greek word for "salvation" is *sozo*. This important word contains the meanings of two English words. It can be translated as either "salvation" or "healing." Let us look at two verses where this word is used. When Jesus healed the woman with the issue of blood He told her, *"...your faith has healed [sozo] you"* (Mark 5:34). Right before Jesus ascended into heaven He told the disciples, *"Whoever believes...will be saved [sozo]"* (Mark 16:16). Both of these verses have the word *sozo* in them; the first verse translates *sozo* as healed, and the second verse translates *sozo* as saved.

Sozo carries two powerful meanings. If we ignore part of the meaning in any given context, we lose a portion of what the New Testament writers are trying to say. I believe almost every time this word is found in the Bible, it should be translated as both saved and healed. Let us insert both meanings into some popular verses to see how this translates into blessings for us.

* When Jesus healed ten lepers, only one of them returned to thank Him. Jesus said to the man, *"Rise and go; your faith has healed you and saved you"* (Luke 17:19).
* *"Everyone who calls on the name of the Lord will be saved and healed"* (Acts 2:21).
* *"Salvation and healing are found in no one else, for there is no other name under heaven given to men by which we must be saved and healed"* (Acts 4:12).
* *"It is by grace you have been saved and healed, through faith and this not from yourselves, it is the gift of God"* (Ephesians 2:8).
* God *"wants all men to be saved and healed and to come to a knowledge of the truth"* (1 Timothy 2:4).

By including the full meaning of the word *sozo* in these translations, we have discovered some powerful healing scriptures. Jesus is in the business of both saving people from sin and healing people from the effects of sin. His title "Savior of the world" also means "Healer of the world."

Jesus bore our sins and sicknesses
   Healing is just as much a part of the atonement as forgiveness of sins. Isaiah emphasizes this fact in his wonderful prophecy concerning the coming Messiah. He says, *"Surely he took up our infirmities and carried our sorrows, yet we considered him stricken by God, smitten by him, and afflicted. But he was pierced for our transgressions, he was crushed for our iniquities; the punishment that brought us peace was upon him, and by his wounds we are healed"* (Isaiah 53:4-5).
   When Isaiah says Jesus "took up" our infirmities he uses the same Hebrew word *nasa* that he uses in Isaiah 53:12 to say Jesus "bore" the sin of many. Many churches preach about how Jesus bore our sins on the cross, but not every church preaches the truth that Jesus also bore our sicknesses when He died on the cross. He carried our sorrows and pains, our sicknesses and diseases, and all our sins to the cross. He died in our place and took all sickness upon His body. Jesus is our substitute; because of His wounds, we can be healed.
   This verse is confirmed in the New Testament. Matthew 8:16-17 reports on the many healings Jesus performed and explains, *"This was to fulfill what was spoken through the prophet Isaiah: "He took up our infirmities and carried our diseases."* Since Jesus bore our sicknesses once, there is no need for us to bear them again.
   Peter also quotes from Isaiah *"He himself bore our sins in his body on the tree, so that we might die to sins and live for righteousness; by his wounds you have been healed"* (1 Peter 2:24). Peter puts this promise in the past tense which means you have already been healed. Two thousand years ago you were healed, the price has already been paid, now all you have to do is claim what is rightfully

yours. The devil has no right to put sickness on you. You are already healed.

The healing power of the blood

It is by the wounds or *"stripes"* of Jesus that we are healed. The stripes Jesus took upon His back were painful. The Roman soldiers tied Him to a whipping post and gave Him thirty-nine lashes with a cat-of-nine-tails. This leather whip had several cords attached to the end, to which were tied shards of glass, sharp rocks, and bits of metal. The whip literally ripped the flesh off of Jesus' back and by the time the flogging was finished, His back must have looked like raw hamburger. Jesus endured hurt and humiliation for the sake of our healing. Do not tell me healing is a side issue for Jesus. By suffering tremendous pain He paid a price too high to calculate, in order to buy our healing.

The blood Jesus shed on the cross paid the price for our sins. The blood Jesus shed when the whip was breaking His body purchased our healing. Both are essential parts of the atonement.

As Christians, we celebrate communion in order to remember what Jesus accomplished on the cross. The wine represents the shedding of His blood which was for the remission of sins. The bread represents the breaking of His body for physical healing. Paul told the Corinthian church that some of their number were becoming sick and even dying because they were taking communion "unworthily." Perhaps many of them were falling sick because they failed to recognize that the body of the Lord was bruised for the sake of their healing.

Each Christian is part of the body of Christ. If one part of the body is hurting, the entire body hurts. As we take communion, we become one with Christ's body. Since Jesus wants His entire body to be healthy, communion is a powerful means to tap into His healing power.

Today some are not healed because they do not fully understand the two-fold meaning of the atonement. Jesus paid the price for both forgiveness and healing, but some only have faith to accept the forgiveness of sins. It is like God has given the church a Christmas tree with many presents under it, but some members of the church only choose to open up the present of "salvation." God has provided healing for every believer, but some leave the gift of "healing" under the tree unwrapped. It is time to unwrap all the gifts of God! The prophet said, *"Heal me, O LORD, and I will be healed; save me and I will be saved..."* (Jeremiah 17:14).

Since healing has not been preached as much as salvation has been preached, faith for healing has not been ignited in as many hearts. But, I believe all this is going to change. As more ministers preach on healing, I believe the church will experience greater healing miracles than ever before!

The Healing Power of
Positive Confession

D id you know every word you speak is important? The words
you confess with your mouth can bring health and healing or
death and destruction. According to Proverbs 18:21, *"The tongue
has the power of life and death..."* Tomorrow's realities are con-
tained in the seed of today's words.

How important are the words we speak? Romans 10:9 says,
*"...if you confess with your mouth, "Jesus is Lord," and believe in
your heart that God raised him from the dead, you will be saved."*
Verbally speaking Christ's Lordship over your life is a vital part of
receiving salvation. Paul goes on to say, *"For it is with your heart
that you believe and are justified, and it is with your mouth that you
confess and are saved"* (Romans 10:10). The confession of your
mouth brings salvation.

Confession is also a vital part of receiving healing. Your tongue
has the power of life and death. If you speak positive words of life,
you will be infused with supernatural life.

Confession is using God's words to describe your situation.
When God sees your pain, He says "By the stripes of Jesus, you
are healed." The moment God notices your sickness, He declares,
"I sent my word to heal your disease." Whenever God hears a cry
for help from a sick person, He answers, "I am the God who heals
you."

Confession is speaking with your mouth what you believe in your heart. Jesus said, *"...out of the overflow of the heart the mouth speaks"* (Matthew 12:34). According to Paul, the word of faith should be in your heart and in your mouth (See Romans 10:8). The best way to have the word of faith in our mouths is to speak the word of God.

It is not a hypocritical lie to confess your healing when you are still sick. In God's eyes, your healing has already been accomplished, and by speaking words of faith rather than words of doubt, you are agreeing with a higher authority. If someone asks you how you are feeling, tell them, "God's healing power is working in my body."

Bad Back Healed

A man in Tulsa, Oklahoma, gave this testimony, "I was in a car accident recently. My car was rear-ended by another vehicle and as a result my back was severely messed up. The doctors told me my situation was hopeless but after listening to Daniel King's teaching for a week, the pain is gone and my back has been completely healed!"

Agree with God and say, "I am healed by the stripes of Jesus (1 Peter 2:24); God is sending His word to heal me (Psalm 107:20); my healing will quickly appear (Isaiah 58:8); this sickness will not end in death (John 11:4); God is taking this sickness away from me (Exodus 23:25); I serve a God who is healing all my diseases (Psalm 103:3).

Confession brings possession

Confession of God's promises brings possession of His promises. Say what God says. Declare the truth that God has already spoken. Use your lips to declare God's will for your life. Speak words of faith, not words of doubt.

It is impossible to be lifted above your confession. Your life will be raised or lowered to the level of your words. Speaking words of doubt shut God out and then begin to let Satan in. Bosworth says, "Disease gains the ascendancy when you confess the testimony of your senses. Feelings and appearances have no place in the realm of faith. Confessing disease is like signing for a package that the express company has delivered. Satan then has the receipt from you showing you have accepted it."

If a mailman brought a box of rattlesnakes to your house, you would not have to accept it. The mailman would try to get you to sign for the snakes because your name is on the package, but if you do not sign, you do not have to accept them and he would be forced to take them away. Gordon Lindsay says, "Symptoms may appear, but you do not have to accept them."

Confessing words of doubt is like signing for the sickness that Satan is trying to give you. If you refuse to confess you are sick, you are rejecting the devil's package. Give no place to the devil; never accept anything he brings.

When a policeman arrests people, he is required to tell them, "Anything you say can be used against you in a court of law." A person's words can legally be presented as evidence during a trial. If your words are important in this world's system, how much more important are your words in the spiritual realm?

Those who overcome the devil do so by *"the blood of the Lamb and by the word of their testimony"* (Revelation 12:11). It is as if in your spiritual life, you are on trial. Satan, the prosecuting attorney, has spoken horrible words of sickness against you. Jesus, the defense attorney, has spoken words of life on your behalf. The judge is leaning over the bench asking, "How do you plead?" If your words agree with Satan's lies, you will be held in captivity, but if your words line up with the words of Jesus, you will be set free!

"How do you plead?" the judge asks again.

"I plead the blood of Jesus which heals me of every sickness," you answer.

The gavel falls. Case closed. You are healed because of your confession!

The Healing Power of the Name of Jesus

The name of Jesus is above every other name in the universe. The name of Jesus is greater than cancer, diabetes, arthritis, AIDS, heart disease, infection, blindness, deafness, and every other sickness ever discovered. This story from Acts chapters 3-4 demonstrates the power of the name of Jesus better than any other story in the Bible.

One day Peter and John were going up to the temple to pray, when they saw a man who had been crippled from birth. Every day this man would sit at the temple gates begging for money.

"Give me some money, please give me some money," asked the crippled man when he saw Peter and John.

They both looked at him and Peter said, "Look at us!" Excited, the man gave them his full attention because he expected them to give him some coins.

Then Peter said, "Silver or gold I do not have..."

The man's face dropped, "It's just my luck to ask a poor person for money," he thought to himself. But then his ears perked back up as he realized Peter was not finished speaking yet.

"...but what I do have, I give you. <u>In the name of Jesus Christ of Nazareth, walk,</u>" commanded Peter. He did not have any money to give the man, but he did possess the healing power that is in the name of Jesus.

Suddenly the crippled man felt blood rush into his legs. He could feel them for the first time in years. He looked up and saw Peter reaching out his hand, and without thinking he grasped the outstretched hand and stood up. Instantly his feet and ankles became strong.

Hesitantly he took a step, then he took another step, and another step. He was walking! He began walking faster, then he tried to hop up and down. Finally he ran around the temple court shouting "Praise God," and showing everyone how he could walk and leap. The crowd in the temple court was astonished because they all recognized him as the man who was once crippled.

Peter asked the crowd who came running, "Men of Israel, why does this surprise you? Why do you stare at us as if we made this man walk through our own power? Through <u>faith in the name of Jesus</u> this man whom you see and know was made strong."

When the priests arrived, they were greatly disturbed because the apostles were talking about how Jesus rose from the dead. They commanded the captain of the temple guard to place them under arrest. The next day all the rulers, elders and teachers of the law asked Peter and John, "By what power or <u>what name did you heal this crippled man?</u>" These men knew Peter did not have any power on his own, so they asked this question in order to discover whose power was behind the miracle.

"It is by <u>the name of Jesus Christ of Nazareth</u>, whom you crucified but whom God raised from the dead, that this man stands before you healed," Peter answered. "Salvation is found in no one else, for there is <u>no other name</u> under heaven given to men by which we must be saved."

The rulers were deeply disturbed because the apostles were preaching and healing people in the name of Jesus, so <u>they commanded them not to speak or teach at all in the name of Jesus.</u> But in a prayer meeting later that night, Peter disobeyed their command and asked God, "Stretch out your hand to heal and perform miraculous signs and wonders through <u>the name of your holy servant Jesus.</u>" After they prayed, the Holy Spirit fell, and all who were at the meeting began to speak the Word of God with great boldness. As they preached, many people in the city of Jerusalem were saved and healed because of the power of the name of Jesus.

Several weeks later, the rulers arrested the apostles once again and accused them, "We gave you strict orders not to teach in this name, yet you continue to preach and heal people in <u>the name of Jesus.</u>" Why did the disciples continue to preach the name of Jesus even though they had been warned not to? It was because they knew the power that exists in the name of Jesus. Peter refused to stop using the name of Jesus because he remembered the words of Jesus, *"...I tell you the truth, my Father will give you whatever you ask in my name. Until now you have not asked for anything in my name. Ask and you will receive, and your joy will be complete"* (John 16:23-24).

There is infinite power in the name of Jesus because His name represents God's omnipotence. When an ambassador speaks to the ruler of a foreign nation, the ambassador's words are backed up by all the power of his nation because he is speaking in the name of his country. When a Christian speaks in the name of Jesus, the believer is backed up by all the power of heaven because we are ambassadors for Christ (2 Corinthians 5:20). As Christians, we have no inherent ability to heal disease, rather, we act under the authority of Jesus. All our authority comes when we act under the authority of the name of Jesus.

Power of an Attorney

If you go on a long, international trip, you can give a friend the "power of attorney" over your personal business. This gives your friend the legal right to conduct your affairs during your absence. He or she would have the ability to access all your bank accounts, pay your bills, sell your property, and sign contracts for you. Your friend would be acting on your behalf, in your name, and under your authority. Your friend's signature would carry all the power of your signature.

When Jesus left earth, He gave Christians the "power of attorney" over His affairs. This means we can do anything Jesus did. Jesus gave us the authority to use His name! When we pray, we are not asking according to our authority, but according to the authority of Jesus.

We are specifically instructed to use the power of the name of Jesus when we pray for the sick. Jesus said, *"And these signs will accompany those who believe: In my name they will...place their hands on sick people, and they will get well"* (Mark 16:17-18).

The "power of attorney" is only as valuable as the assets backing up the name. What assets does the name of Jesus represent? The name of Jesus is above every other name. Someday every knee will bow at the sound of His name (Philippians 2:9-10). The name of Jesus is above every demon. The name of Jesus is above every sickness. The name of Jesus is above every other name ever uttered.

His name represents *"incomparably great power for us who believe"* (Ephesians 1:19). Both salvation and healing are found in the name of Jesus. *"Everyone who calls on the name of the Lord will be saved"* (Acts 2:21). There is no other name under heaven given to us by which we can be saved (Acts 4:12). Do you want to be saved from sin? Call on the name of Jesus. Do you want to be saved from sickness? Call on the name of Jesus. The name of Jesus stands for full provision, infinite wisdom, ultimate power, and complete healing. The name of Jesus can procure anything in the universe.

When a policeman pulls you over, he is not acting under his own authority. Once he is off duty he has no right to stop you for speeding, but when he is dressed in his uniform, he is acting in the name of the government. When we are clothed with the power of the Holy Spirit, we are not walking in our own insignificant authority, but in the overwhelming authority of Jesus. When we use the name of Jesus, we walk in all the authority of Jesus. It is as if Jesus Himself is present. Where two or three come together in the name of Jesus, He is there in the midst of them (Matthew 18:19-20).

Jesus said, *"...I will do whatever you ask in my name.... You may ask me for anything in my name, and I will do it"* (John 14:13-14). Does "anything" include asking for healing from sickness? You can bet your last dollar it does. Jesus promised, *"I will do whatever you ask in my name."* Stop reading right now and ask for healing in the name of Jesus; the power in the name guarantees your healing.

The Healing Power of God's Word

In the beginning was the Word. The Word was with God and the Word was God. Jesus, the Word of God became flesh and dwelt among us. God sent forth His Word to heal our diseases (Psalm 107:20). When the incarnate Word walked on earth, He healed sickness.

God sent His Son for a season, but He left His written word for all eternity. Treat the word of God with the same respect you would show Jesus if He walked into your room. The word has the same power to heal today as Jesus had when he was physically present.

Originally the world was created at God's spoken command. *"Through faith we understand that the worlds were framed by the word of God, so that things which are seen were not made of things which do appear"* (Hebrews 11:3 KJV). If the word of God can create the mighty galaxies, then it can recreate the cells in our bodies.

The word of God brings healing. Wise King Solomon says the words of God *"...are life unto those that find them, and health to all their flesh"* (Proverbs 4:22 KJV). The psalmist sings *"...Your word has given me life"* (Psalm 119:50 NKJV).

The word of God is both a defensive and an offensive weapon. In Ephesians 6, we discover that faith is like a shield that is capable of quenching every fiery arrow of the evil one. Well, where does faith come from? Faith comes from hearing God's word. As soon you hear the word of God, it becomes a defensive shield that protects you from the attacks of Satan.

The word of God is also called the Sword of the Spirit (Ephesians 6:17). The Christian who speaks God's word with boldness is like the ancient hero who wielded his sword in great arcs against his enemy. The word is a sharp and effective weapon. When you speak God's word it destroys the works of Satan.

The word is living and powerful. God personally guarantees His word. Every word ever spoken by God must come true. All the promises of God are "yes" and "Amen." When God speaks it, it is so.

God's word is settled for all of eternity in heaven (Psalm 119:89), and He carefully watches to see that His word is fulfilled (Jeremiah 1:12). The word is eternal, it is unchanging, it is the will of God. *"The word of the Lord stands forever"* (1 Peter 1:25), it will never pass away (Matthew 24:35).

The good news in God's word does not change like the bad news in your daily newspaper. Every day brings a new headline in the news, but God's word stands the test of time: unchanging, solid, and immovable. God's word is more solid than a doctor's report concerning your health. The report of a doctor can change, but God's word will never be altered.

One word from God will change your life forever

You are only one verse away from receiving your healing. If you will grab hold of one of God's promises and memorize it, confess it, and claim it as your own, you can be healed.

Let me share a story that illustrates the power of one word. One evening Jesus told His disciples to get in a boat and to cross to the other side of the sea. Later, when Jesus wanted to rejoin them, He walked on the water to their boat. The disciples were scared and wondered if a ghost was approaching them. Knowing their fear, Jesus cried out to them, "Be of good cheer! It is I; do not be afraid."

Peter, ever one to take action, called back, "Lord, if it is you, command me to come out on the water." Jesus replied with one simple word, "Come." Immediately, Peter hopped out of the boat and walked toward Jesus.

Any one of the disciples could have walked on the water. Jesus did not say, "Peter, come" He simply said, "Come." All the disciples could have jumped out of the boat and played a game of football on the water just on the basis of that one word. In sermons we often criticize Peter for sinking after taking his eyes off Jesus, but we need to give him a break; he was the only disciple with the guts to step out on the water. At least he had the faith to give walking on the water a try, the other disciples just stayed in the comfortable boat as spectators.

On the basis of one word from Jesus, Peter defied the laws of gravity. Because of faith in one word, Peter stepped out of the boat and into the pages of the Bible. All you need is faith in one word from God to receive your complete healing.

The Healing Power of Prayer

" *Is any one of you sick? He should call the elders of the church to pray over him and anoint him with oil in the name of the Lord. And the prayer offered in faith will make the sick person well; the Lord will raise him up. If he has sinned, he will be forgiven. Therefore confess your sins to each other and pray for each other so that you may be healed. The prayer of a righteous man is powerful and effective"* (James 5:14-16).

There are many elements of healing found in this passage including: calling the elders of the church, anointing with oil, praying in the name of Jesus, the prayer of faith, and the power of confessing sins. But the element I want to focus on right now is an important ingredient in the healing process. This vital element is prayer.

The prayer of a righteous person is powerful and effective (James 5:16). The prayer of the upright pleases God (Proverbs 15:8). The Lord hears the prayer of the righteous (Proverbs 15:29). The eyes of the Lord are on the righteous and his ears are attentive to their prayer (1 Peter 3:12). This means the prayer of a person in right standing with God can achieve great miracles.

Prayer literally opens the door into the throne room of God. Someone once said, "The amount of power in your life is determined by the size of the calluses on your knees." I like to say, "If you want to be feeling your healing, you need to be kneeling for your healing to stop Satan from stealing your healing." Prayer has the potential to move heaven and earth on your behalf. John Wesley observed, "It seems God is limited by our prayer life - that He can do nothing for humanity unless someone asks Him."

Sonogram Proves Tumors are Gone

A woman in Belo Horizonte, Brazil, testified, "The doctors found four tumors on my ovaries. After the service last night, I prayed and asked God to heal me. This morning, I visited the doctor for another sonogram and he discovered that the tumors have completely disappeared!"

What is prayer? Prayer is simply talking with God. It is fellowship with your Heavenly Father. Prayer is the single most important activity you could engage in. Prayer is evidence of your trust in God. F.B. Myer said, "The great tragedy of life is not unanswered prayer, but unoffered prayer." There is nothing greater than speaking with the Creator of the universe.

The psalmist said, *"...God has surely listened and heard my voice in prayer. Praise be to God, who has not rejected my prayer..."* (Psalm 66:19-20). Jesus promised, *"If you believe, you will receive whatever you ask for in prayer"* (Matthew 21:22), and again, *"...whatever you ask for in prayer, believe that you have received it, and it will be yours"* (Mark 11:24).

Every time Satan attacks your mind with thoughts of doubt and unbelief, defend yourself by going to the Lord in prayer. *"Do not be anxious about anything, but in everything, by prayer and petition, with thanksgiving, present your requests to God"* (Philippians 4:6). Do not worry about sickness. Bring your healing request to the Lord through prayer, give thanks for your healing, and you will be made whole. I agree with William Branham, "He who is a stranger to prayer is a stranger to power."

Daniel King

Four ways to pray for healing

1. Pray for yourself.
Building your faith through personal prayer is the secret to obtaining and maintaining your healing.

2. Ask a family member to pray for you.
Parents' prayers are especially effective when praying for their children because God has given them authority to resist Satan's attacks in their household.

3. Call for the elders of your church to pray for you.
"Is any one of you sick? He should call the elders of the church to pray over him..." (James 5:14). Ask an elder to pray over you; when his faith combines with your faith, you will be healed.

4. Ask a friend to agree with you.
"Again, I tell you that if two of you on earth agree about anything you ask for, it will be done for you by my Father in heaven. For where two or three come together in my name, there am I with them" (Matthew 18:19-20). There is great power when two people pray a prayer of agreement.

46

The Healing Power of
Laying On of Hands

When I pray for the sick, I frequently feel God's anointing in my right hand. When this happens, I quickly lay my hands on the sick person. The anointing produces a burning sensation in my hand, and as I pray I can literally feel power flow from the Spirit of God inside of me into the diseased body.

Why is laying hands on the sick so important? Laying hands on the sick serves as a point of contact that allows God's power to be transferred. In this story we see how Jesus used His hands to bring healing.

One day a ruler of the synagogue named Jairus fell at the feet of Jesus and begged for help. The crowd around Jesus thought this was a strange sight because normally such an important man would not plead for assistance, but Jairus was desperate. He told Jesus, "My little daughter is dying. Please come and lay your hands on her so that she will be healed and live." As Jesus looked into the man's tear filled eyes, He felt compassion; so, He followed him towards his house.

On the way to Jairus' home Jesus was delayed because a desperate woman came to Him for healing. When they finally arrived, it was too late. Some men came and told Jairus, "Your daughter is dead. Don't bother the teacher any more."

Of course Jesus ignored their bad news and encouraged the synagogue ruler, "Don't be afraid; just believe." The people around the house were crying loudly because of the death. Jesus asked them not to cry and added, "The child is not dead but asleep." But they laughed in His face because everyone knew the child was already dead.

Jesus was able to say this because He already knew the end of the story. Did you know Jesus never preached a funeral? As a matter of fact, He spoiled every funeral He ever went to, including His own.

Jesus left the crowd outside and entered the room where the dead girl was lying. He touched her hand with His hand and gently whispered, "Little girl, I say to you, get up." The moment Jesus touched the girl's hand, she rose from the dead. Immediately she stood up from her death bed and hugged her excited parents.

The key point I want you to notice in this story is that Jairus asked Jesus to lay His hands on his daughter. You see, Jairus knew the power of a personal touch. As soon as the hands of Jesus touched the hands of the dead girl, power entered her body and she was completely healed. The hands of Jesus contain healing power.

When a leper came to Jesus for healing, Jesus reached out His hand and touched him (Mark 1:40-41). On the surface this was not a smart thing to do because leprosy is highly contagious; if you touch a leper, you can catch leprosy. So why did Jesus touch this man? Jesus knew the healing power in His hand was stronger than the leprosy.

Another time, *"When the sun was setting, the people brought to Jesus all who had various kinds of sickness, and laying his hands on each one, he healed them"* (Luke 4:40). In the hometown of Jesus, He laid hands on people as He healed them (Mark 6:5).

Paul also laid his hands on the sick. On the island of Malta, the father of the chief official of the island was suffering from fever and dysentery. As Paul prayed, he laid his hands on the sick man and he was completely healed (Acts 28:8).

Right before Jesus returned to heaven, He commanded His disciples to *"place their hands on sick people,"* and He promised, *"they will get well"* (Mark 16:18). As Christians we have been given both a command and a promise. If we will do our part by laying hands on the sick, God will do His part and heal them!

PRESCRIPTION FOR HEALTH

"...by his wounds you have been healed"
(1 Peter 2:24)

Dr. Jesus

The Healing Power of
Anointing With Oil

A nother element of healing power is anointing with oil. *"Is any one of you sick? He should call the elders of the church to pray over him and anoint him with oil..."* (James 5:14).

Everyone remembers the familiar words of Psalm 23, *"The LORD is my shepherd, I shall not be in want.... You anoint my head with oil...."* David, the author of this psalm, was a shepherd as a boy. He knew that before a shepherd puts his sheep to sleep at night, he carefully checks them for injuries and rubs oil on their wounds. This anointing oil prevented the sheep's wounds from becoming infected and protected them from annoying insects.

Jesus said, *"I am the good shepherd..."* (John 10:14). Today's pastors follow in His footsteps by becoming shepherds for their congregations. Good shepherds desire for their sheep to be free from injury. When the elders of the church pray for the sick, they are told to use anointing oil. I believe the anointing oil symbolically represents the oil a shepherd would use to heal his sheep.

Oil also represents the healing presence of the Holy Spirit. In some of the parables of Jesus, the Holy Spirit is symbolized by oil. When anointing oil is used in praying for the sick, it represents the presence of the Holy Spirit; so, the elders of the church are not praying alone, they are praying along with the Spirit.

If you are sick, call the elders of your church to come pray for you. Ask them to anoint you with oil and to lay their hands on you. Their prayer of faith will be powerful and effective in bringing the Spirit's healing anointing to your body.

The Healing Power of the Gifts of Healing

" *To one there is given through the Spirit...gifts of healing...* " (1 Corinthians 12:8-9). One of the nine gifts of the Spirit is healing. Every child of God can heal the sick through faith in Jesus, but some Christians are given a specific gift for healing the sick.

In the body of Christ there are many needs. God has provided for every need by giving a member of the body a gift to meet the need. One of the greatest needs is healing, and God has placed many people in the body who have a special anointing to believe for healing.

The *"gifts of healing"* are plural. This means there is more than one gift of healing. God has given some people tremendous faith to believe for certain healings. Everyone has a measure of faith, but I believe some people are specially gifted to believe for certain miracles.

There have been many great healing evangelists in the last one hundred years. Each of them was given a special gift to believe for healing. Some healings occur because of faith in the heart of the sick person, but other healings happen because of the faith of a preacher. After a preacher has seen thousands of healings, he is better equipped to know how to deal with a particular case of sickness.

Many doctors and nurses have also been given a healing gift. The desire to make people well sustains them through years of medical school when others without the gift drop out. Their spiritual gift for healing helps them seek a natural means to heal the sick.

Someone who has fought a particular disease and won will have an advantage when praying for others with that disease. God gives the healed person a gift in the area of their miracle. Experiencing healing in one's own life builds faith for healing others.

I think there are as many gifts for healing as there are diseases. Within the body of Christ, God has provided a solution to every disease. Someone is gifted in the area of your greatest need. As you seek God, He will reveal a person with the answer to your problem.

So, in your quest for healing, look for those who have been given a gift of healing. When their faith is added to your faith, you will have the perfect climate for a miracle.

The Healing Power of Authority and Power

L ong before nations were called "superpowers" there existed a real super power. This is the power of God that is mightier than any other power on earth. Let's look at what the scriptures say about God's power and its ability to heal your body.

The power of God can be compared to electric power. Electricity is a dynamic force which has radically changed our civilization by providing us with light and heat. After this power is generated by huge powerhouses, it flows along electric lines until it reaches an outlet in your house. The electricity is always present in that outlet, but it does not do you any good unless you plug an appliance into the outlet.

Healing power is similar to electric power. God is the supernatural powerhouse, and our faith is the wire that connects us to His power. God's anointing is always present, but it does us no good unless we plug into it.

Electricity is real whether you believe in it or not; in the same way, God's power is real whether you believe in it or not. If you refuse to believe in electricity and do not plug your toaster into an outlet, you will eat bread instead of toast for breakfast. Similarly unbelief stops the flow of God's power.

A "point of contact" is like an electric outlet; it is the place where one uses faith to tap into God's power. An outlet with nothing plugged into it is useless. God's power, knowledge, and capability is everywhere and it is always available, but unless someone uses faith to connect to the power, the power is wasted.

The power of God is present to heal your body right now. Use your faith to "connect" with God's powerhouse to receive your healing.

What is the difference between power and authority?

"When Jesus had called the Twelve together, he gave them power and authority to drive out all demons and to cure diseases" (Luke 9:1). In this verse we discover Jesus gives His disciples both power and authority to heal the sick. What is the difference between power and authority?

The word "power" is translated from the Greek word *dunamis.* To get an idea of the meaning of this word, we need to imagine the most powerful forces on earth. Our English word "dynamite" is derived from this potent word. Electric power, nuclear power, and massive explosions all express the sense of this word.

Dunamis power is the type of power that flowed from Jesus when the woman with the issue of blood touched Him. The power was a literal substance that went out of Jesus into the body of the women and healed her. Jesus actually felt an explosion of *dunamis* power leave His body in response to her faith.

The word "authority" is from the Greek word *exousia.* This second word is actually a term used in a courtroom to describe legal rights. A policeman has the authority to give a ticket to a speeder. A judge has the authority to send a criminal to prison. The President has the authority to wage war on another country.

Jesus claimed absolute authority when He said, *"All authority in heaven and on earth has been given to me"* (Matthew 28:18). Jesus was given the legal right to use any of God's infinite resources in His battle with the devil. In turn, He fully authorized His disciples to walk in the same authority. The authority of Jesus was birthed in His relationship with His Father, and the authority of the disciples

Mohammad the Cripple

Our team experienced many problems in setting up a healing festival in Metu, Ethiopia. Many Muslims lived in the area and some of the Muslim young people followed our publicity team and tore down all our posters. One day, they actually started a riot and threw a stone through the front windshield of our publicity vehicle. When the police came, the Muslims lied and said our team had started the riot. Eighteen of our team members were thrown into jail and we had to hire a lawyer to get them out.

Because of this opposition, we were greatly disappointed with the first night's attendance. But on the second night a miracle happened that changed everything. Someone brought a crippled Muslim man named Mohammad to the festival. When we began to pray for the sick, Jesus touched Mohammad the cripple and healed him.

He came running up on the platform holding his crutch high into the air yelling, "I can walk. Jesus healed me." I asked, "What is your name?" He replied, "My name is Mohammad." Because of his name, the entire crowd realized that he was a Muslim. Word began to spread across the city, "Jesus is healing the Muslims." The next night, the crowd size doubled. The next night, attendance doubled again. By the final night of the festival, over 55,000 people gathered on the field, many of them were Muslims hearing that Jesus can heal for the first time.

originated in their relationship with Jesus. Authority always comes from relationship.

Both power and authority are important. Owning a gun can give you the power to kill, but just possessing a gun does not necessarily give you the authority to use the gun. A policeman is given special permission to use his gun; in other words, he has both the power (the ability) and the authority (the legal right) to protect the innocent.

In my seventh grade science class, I studied two different types of energy. Potential energy is stored energy. A rock sitting on top of a cliff is full of potential energy. But when the rock is pushed off the edge of the cliff, the potential energy is transformed into kinetic energy, the energy of movement. *Exousia* is like potential energy; it gives Jesus the potential right to heal. *Dunamis* power is like kinetic energy; it gives Jesus the ability to heal.

Jesus gave the disciples both the power (*dunamis* power) and the authority (*exousia* power) to heal people. God has given you both the ability to defeat Satan and the legal right to make your power hold.

The infinite power of God

The prophet wrote, *"Ah, Sovereign LORD, you have made the heavens and the earth by your great power and outstretched arm. Nothing is too hard for you"* (Jeremiah 32:17). If God made the earth by His power and uses the same power to keep the stars in their places, don't you think this power is able to heal your body? (Jeremiah 10:12; Isaiah 40:26).

According to Acts 10:38, God anointed Jesus with the Holy Spirit and power. Jesus used this power to go around doing good and to heal all who were under the power of the devil. The power of Jesus is far stronger than the power of Satan.

Everywhere Jesus went, He was filled with the power of the Spirit (Luke 4:14). Supernatural power enabled Him to cast out evil spirits (Luke 4:36) and was present when Jesus healed the sick (Luke 5:17). When the crowds touched Jesus, power flowed from within Him and healed them all (Luke 6:19).

Jesus promised to clothe us with the same *"power from on high"* (Luke 24:49). This promise was given again in Acts 1:8, *"...You will receive power when the Holy Spirit comes on you..."* On the day of Pentecost, Holy Spirit power fell from heaven (Acts 2:1-4). As Christians, we now have the power to *"overcome all the power of the enemy"* (Luke 10:19). We can use this power to cast out demons and to cure diseases (Luke 9:1).

Paul fully proclaimed the gospel by using the power of the Spirit to perform signs and wonders (Romans 15:19). Paul was not ashamed of the gospel because it is the power of God for both salvation and healing for everyone who believes (Romans 1:16). His preaching was not with wise and persuasive words, but with a demonstration of the Spirit's power (1 Corinthians 2:4); *"for the kingdom of God is not a matter of talk but of power"* (1 Corinthians 4:20).

Jesus rebuked the religious leaders of His day for not knowing the Scriptures or the power of God (Matthew 22:29). Some Christians today have a form of godliness, but they deny its power. Paul tells us to *"have nothing to do with them"* (2 Timothy 3:5). Never listen to anyone who tells you God does not have the power to heal you today.

The Healing Power of Rebuking the Devil

S atan comes to steal, kill, and destroy (John 10:10). One way
the devil accomplishes his evil designs is by oppressing people
with sickness. In the Bible, we discover some sicknesses are even
directly caused by demon possession. The good news is that it does
not really matter whether a sickness is the result of natural causes or
demonic causes. The name of Jesus has power over both!

While Jesus was on top of the Mount of Transfiguration, a man
brought his son to the disciples. The boy was suffering from seizures
caused by demonic oppression. The father was extremely worried
about his son because the demon threw the child into fires trying to
burn him and into water trying to drown him. The disciples tried to
heal the boy but they were unable to do so. When Jesus returned, He
scolded them for their lack of faith.

Jesus called the boy to Him and rebuked the demon. At that
moment, the boy was healed. Later the disciples asked Jesus why
they were unable to heal the boy. Jesus blamed their failure on their
lack of faith, but He did give them a way to build their faith when He
said, *"...this kind [of demon] does not go out except by prayer and
fasting"* (Matthew 17:21).

Some types of demonic attack are so vicious, we need a period
of time to build our faith before we can defeat Satan. Fasting is when
one abstains from eating food in order to spend time in prayer. By
denying the insistent demands of your body, you can be completely

focused on worshiping God. This period of fasting will build your faith to believe for God's healing power!

Notice, Jesus rebuked the demon and cast it out. The authority of Jesus was far stronger than the demon's hold over this young boy's life. When Jesus rebuked the demon, the evil spirit was forced to leave.

Time after time in the Gospels, Jesus set people free from demonic power. One day Jesus was stepping out of a boat when a violent demon-infested man appeared. He was so crazy that he refused to wear clothes, and he lived in a graveyard. Repeatedly officials had tried to control him by locking him in chains, but the man would break the chains and run away.

Jesus asked the man, "What is your name?"

"Legion," the man replied, because many demons lived inside him. A legion was a term used by the Romans to describe a six thousand-man army. This man's sickness was caused by a horde of demonic powers.

One day as I was reading this story, I asked myself, "How can six thousand demons fit inside one person?" I realized the spiritual world operates under a different set of rules than the physical world. I am not sure if this man literally had thousands of demons possessing him, but I do know a lot of demons were involved. If the human spirit can be oppressed by a legion of demons, the good news is that there is plenty of room for the same human spirit to be filled with the Holy Spirit. As Christians our spirits can be filled with an enormous amount of the Spirit's power. We can have more than enough power to handle every demonic threat.

Jesus commanded the evil spirits to come out of the man and to go into a nearby herd of pigs (Luke 8:32-33). The pigs went crazy because of the demons and rushed over a cliff and drowned in the lake. But the man was completely healed because of the authority of Jesus!

Jesus gave this same authority to us. We can *"drive out evil spirits and...heal every disease and sickness"* (Matthew 10:1). Jesus commanded, *"Heal the sick...drive out demons..."* (Matthew 10:8). He promised, *"...These signs will accompany those who believe: In my name they will drive out demons..."* (Mark 16:17). If we will submit to God and resist the devil, all evil powers will flee at our command (James 4:7). Demonic sickness offers no problems for those filled with God's Spirit!

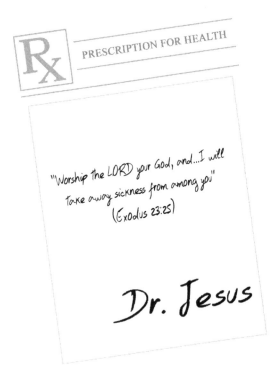

The Healing Power of God's Will

S everal years ago my grandfather died. After his funeral, his will was read to the family. In that will, he expressed his desires concerning the disposal of his worldly goods. The written will established beyond a shadow of a doubt what he wanted to happen to his money.

My grandfather was the testator, the one who set up the will. A lawyer was the mediator or advocate of the will; his job was to guarantee that the conditions of the will were fulfilled. The family members were the beneficiaries of the will, they received the benefits from the estate.

Jesus was a testator; He left his will on earth when He died. In the Bible there is an Old Testament and a New Testament; the word "testament" refers to a will. When Jesus died, He left His last will and testament. In it His will concerning healing was established once and for all.

Once the writer of a will is dead, nothing can be added to the will or subtracted from the will. Jesus clearly expressed His desire concerning healing when He was on earth. Any theology which denies Jesus is willing to heal people today is nothing but a false addition to the will.

Jesus' desires concerning His estate can be found in the New Testament. The words Jesus left behind, in the form of the Bible, perfectly express the will of God concerning His earthly estate. His will can make you well.

What possessions did Jesus leave on earth? His robe was stolen by the soldiers who crucified him, so He did not leave any physical possessions. One item Jesus did possess was the authority to heal the sick. He said, *"All authority in heaven and on earth has been given to me"* (Matthew 28:18). It was this authority to drive out evil spirits and to heal every disease and sickness that He left to His disciples in His will (Matthew 10:1). We are the beneficiaries of Christ's estate. All His authority and power now belongs to us. Jesus bequeathed to us all the promises of God in His will.

When Jesus rose from the dead, He became the advocate or mediator with the Father who guarantees that the conditions of the will are fulfilled. Jesus made His will known before He died, then the resurrected Jesus became the lawyer who ensures that every promise in the will comes to pass. *"...Christ is the mediator of a new covenant, that those who are called may receive the promised eternal inheritance..."* (Hebrews 9:15).

There is only one person in the Bible who questions the will of Jesus to heal. In the first healing story recorded by Matthew, a man with leprosy comes and kneels before Jesus. The man says, "Lord, if you are willing, you can make me clean."

Jesus reveals His will concerning healing to us and quickly reassures the man by gently saying, "I am willing, be clean!" Immediately the man was cured of the leprosy.

Leprosy was a hideous, contagious disease that separated the sick person from society because the leper was not permitted to come within ten feet of those who were well. This prohibition prevented the leper from worshiping God in a synagogue or in the temple. The leprosy effectively severed the leper from the ability to worship God in a community of believers. By healing this man, Jesus restored both his lost relationships and his ability to worship God.

The only way Jesus will ever answer the question, "Are you willing to heal me?" is "Yes, I am willing!"

This is why there is no need to pray the formalistic prayer, "Lord, if it be thy will, you can heal me." You can know beyond a shadow of a doubt, it is God's will to heal you. Asking if it is God's will for you to be healed is an insult to God's promise. God's Word says, "You are healed." God said it once; He does not want to, nor need to, repeat Himself.

T.L. Osborn says, "Not knowing the will of God in a certain matter, we may pray in faith that God will do this for us, if it be His will; and He will do what is best for us. But where God has revealed His will, by promising to do a certain thing, we need not be in ignorance of it or in doubt concerning it."

God desires to heal you. It is written in His will; thus it is settled for all of eternity. God does not want you to be sick; God wants you to be well. God's will has been made known. God's will must not be questioned; it must simply be trusted. The Father wrote it; Jesus guarantees it; and the Spirit brings healing as you believe.

If God wills for all to be healed, why are some not healed? God also *"wants all men to be saved"* (1 Timothy 2:4), but not all are saved. Some are not saved because they do not believe; some are not healed for the same reason.

Jesus was the physical manifestation of God's will. Jesus said, *"...I have come to do your will, O God"* (Hebrews 10:7). Jesus only did the will of His Father. *"For I have come down from heaven not to do my will but to do the will of him who sent me"* (John 6:38). As we read the Gospels, we see God's will unfolding in the activities of Jesus. He acted out God's will concerning healing through His actions. Jesus perfectly revealed the will of God in the area of healing as He opened blind eyes, touched deaf ears, cleansed lepers, and healed cripples. If it was God's will to heal people when Jesus was on earth, it is God's will to heal you today.

PRESCRIPTION FOR HEALTH

"... The Sun of Righteousness shall arise
with healing in His wings..."
(Malachi 4:2 NKJV)

Dr. Jesus

The Healing Power of
God's Presence

G od's presence is the most precious commodity in the universe. David knew this when he begged God, *"Do not cast me from your presence..."* (Psalm 51:11). If you were away from the presence of God for even a fraction of a second, you would cease to exist.

God is omnipresent. This means He is everywhere and in everything. The presence of God holds the atoms together; it maintains the cycle of the seasons; it feeds the sun's energy; it keeps the stars in the sky; and it causes plants to grow. Most important of all, the presence of God brings healing.

Even though God is omnipresent, there are times when we can feel a stronger concentration of His presence in a certain place. For example, Luke records one occasion when *"the power of the Lord was present to heal"* (Luke 5:17). On this particular day, the presence of God's healing power was strong.

One of God's names is Jehovah Rapha, which means, "The Lord who heals." This name reveals that healing is part of the nature of God. He is life and the source of all life. Being in His presence infuses divine life into our mortal bodies. It restores lost muscle tissue, brings peace to troubled minds, refreshes the spirit, cleanses impurities, drives out infection, and forces the organs to function properly.

Never Stop Looking for a Miracle

As people left the festival field, one mother was disappointed. Her four-year-old girl was still unable to walk. She had brought her daughter hoping for a miracle but nothing had happened. Her little girl was still crippled, just as she had been from birth.

After putting her daughter to sleep in her own bedroom, the mother cried herself to sleep. The next morning, she felt a hand on her cheek. Startled, she opened her eyes. Who could be touching her? "Mommy," she heard a voice say. It was her daughter. "How did you get in here?" she asked. "I walked," replied the child. In the middle of the night, Jesus had completely healed her.

Do you like to spend time where you are appreciated? God feels the same way. The best way to invite His presence is to spend time worshiping Him. Often people will be healed when an atmosphere of God's presence is created through worship. The Bible tells us that God inhabits the praises of His people (See Psalm 22:3). When a crescendo of praise and worship reaches heaven, God's presence arrives and along with His presence comes His healing power.

The Lord promised Moses, *"My Presence will go with you, and I will give you rest"* (Exodus 33:14). Moses valued the presence of God so much that he told God, "If your presence does not go with me, I don't even want to go." He knew that in God's presence is joy (Psalm 16:11), rest (Exodus 33:14), safety (Psalm 31:20), blessing (Psalm 89:15), and healing (Luke 5:17), and he refused to go anywhere without God's presence.

The present of healing comes when we spend time in the presence of God Almighty.

The Story of
the Dying King

(2 Kings 20:1-11; 2 Chronicles 30-32; Isaiah 38)

T he king was sick and dying. He looked up at the purple canopy covering his bed and coughed. Despite the lush trappings of his room, nothing could be done for his health. The best doctors money could buy were unable to help him. He had only one hope left, the prophet of the Lord.

The king knew the Lord could heal because when he was a young man, he had reintroduced the Passover to his people. He remembered asking the Lord, during the ceremony, to pardon all those who set their hearts on seeking God. In response the Lord had healed all the people of their illnesses as a sign of His favor.

"King Hezekiah, the prophet Isaiah is coming" one of the worried attendants announced.

When the prophet appeared, the king desperately grabbed his hand, "Give me some good news. Will the Lord heal me?"

Sadly, the prophet stroked the trembling hand of the king, "I am sorry, this is what the Lord says: Put your house in order, because you are going to die; you will not recover."

Shocked, the king jerked his hand out of the prophet's grasp. The man of God had prophesied his imminent death. With his last hope dashed, the king turned his face away from the world and towards the wall. He began to weep bitterly. He had accomplished so much for God and for the nation of Judea, but now all the pride he had in his deeds was swept away as he thought of his desperate situation.

The prophet quietly left shaking his head. Despite his love for this king, he could only prophesy what the Lord told him to say.

During the Passover ceremony, the Lord healed the people because they were seeking Him with all their hearts. Hezekiah decided to begin seeking God. With his face to the wall and tears pouring from his eyes, the king humbled himself and cried out to God, "Remember, O Lord, how I have walked before you faithfully and with wholehearted devotion and have done what is good in your eyes."

The prophet was passing through the middle of the palace's three courts when suddenly, he stopped. The Lord was speaking. Isaiah bent his head as he listened to the message from heaven, "Go back and tell Hezekiah, the leader of my people, 'This is what the Lord, the God of your father David, says: I have heard your prayers and seen your tears; I will heal you. In three days, you will be worshiping at the temple.'" The prophet could not believe his ears; God had changed His mind!

Isaiah turned and ran back to the king's bedroom. "Put some more medicine on the king," he shouted, "He is going to get better."

Scarcely believing his ears, the king turned and wiped the tears away from his eyes, "What will be the sign that I will be healed?" he asked.

On the spur of the moment, the prophet pointed to the sundial outside the window, "Do you want the shadow to go forward ten degrees or backwards ten degrees?"

Hezekiah thought for a second, "The shadow always goes forward. I want to see time go backward ten degrees."

The prophet called upon the Lord, and God made the shadow move backward as a sign. God was willing to literally move heaven and earth for the sake of his servant's request.

Three days later Hezekiah was completely healed, and he went up to the temple to thank the Lord.

Power Points

1. God does not change, yet in this story God seems to change His mind. At first the prophet said Hezekiah was going to die, then he returned and said the king was going to live. What happened? The circumstances affecting God's decision had changed. When Hezekiah humbled himself and reminded God of his devotion, God responded to his faith and declared that he would live. In this story, we find that God is willing to change His mind and move heaven and earth in response to the faith of one of His children.

2. Humbleness before God is essential for your miracle. *"God opposes the proud but gives grace to the humble"* (James 4:6). Hezekiah humbly cried out to God during his greatest time of need. This humble attitude caught God's attention and sparked a miracle. Tears of repentance bring healing.

3. Healing can come through medicine. When Isaiah returned to prophesy about Hezekiah's healing, he told the servants to prepare a medicinal poultice made from figs. After the servants gave him the medicine, the king recovered. Often, God uses medicine to bring healing.

   This concept is also found in the New Testament. Jesus said, *"It is not the healthy who need a doctor, but the sick"* (Matthew 9:12). One of Paul's closest companions was Luke the physician, and Paul told Timothy to drink what could have been medicinal wine for his stomach (1 Timothy 5:23).

PRESCRIPTION FOR HEALTH

"...I will restore you to health and heal your wounds, declares the LORD..."
(Jeremiah 30:17)

Dr. Jesus

Our Goal?
Every Soul!

Daniel & Jessica King

Soul Winning Festivals

Metu, Ethiopia

Khushpur, Pakistan

Roca Blanca, Mexico

Sialkot, Pakistan

Agere Maryam, Ethiopia

Kisaran, Indonesia

The Blind See

The Deaf Hear

Cripples Walk

**Miracles Prove
Jesus is Alive!**

Empty Wheelchair

Set Free From Demons

Lame Walking

Tumor Gone

When Daniel King was fifteen years old, he set a goal to lead 1,000,000 people to Jesus before his 30th birthday. Instead of trying to become a millionaire, he decided to lead a million "heirs" into the kingdom of God. *"If you belong to Christ then you are heirs"* (Galatians 3:29).

After celebrating the completion of this goal, Daniel & Jessica made it their mission to go for one million souls every year.

This **Quest for Souls** is accomplished through:

* Soul Winning Festivals
* Leadership Training
* Literature Distribution
* Humanitarian Relief

Would you help us lead
people to Jesus by joining
The MillionHeir's Club?

Visit www.kingministries.com to get involved!

The Story of
the Healing of an Enemy

(2 Kings 5)

Naaman was a great man. He was the commander of the army of the king of Aram. He was famous throughout his country and feared by the armies of other countries. Because of his military victories, he was wealthy and respected. There was only one small problem with his life; he had the incurable disease of leprosy.

Doctors were unable to cure his sickness. There was no hope. He was doomed to be slowly eaten away by this feared horror, shunned by all his friends because of the contagious skin disease.

One day his wife came to him, "Honey, one of my slave girls told about a man who can heal you."

"Which slave girl is that?" he growled at her.

"The little girl you captured in Israel and gave me as a present. She claims there is a prophet in Samaria who can cure you of leprosy."

"How can anyone in that insignificant country cure me? Here we are far more advanced and none of our doctors can do a thing."

His wife smiled at her husband, "At least give it a try, for my sake."

So, Naaman found himself traveling to the house of the prophet Elisha. As he neared the town where Elisha lived, he imagined the prophet coming out of his house to honor him as a great commander.

"Perhaps the prophet will wave his hand, dance up and down, and call upon his God to heal me," thought Naaman.

Instead, Elisha sent his servant with a message for Naaman, "Go, wash yourself seven times in the Jordan River, and your flesh will be restored and you will be cleansed."

Hopping mad, Naaman rode away in a fury. "We have cleaner rivers where I come from; why should I wash in the dirty little creeks of this country?" he asked his servants.

The servants humbly reminded him, "If Elisha had asked you to do a difficult task in order to be healed, would you have done it?"

"Yes," he answered.

"Then, why don't you obey him when he only asks you to wash yourself seven times?" the servants asked him.

Despite his misgivings, Naaman decided his servants were right. He changed into his bathing suit and began to wash in the river as the man of God had told him to do. The servants cringed at the sight of the ugly leprosy on his body.

He dipped in the water the first time and eagerly examined his skin. Nothing had changed. He dipped for the second time. No change. Three. "If this prophet is wrong, he's going to lose his head," he muttered to himself. Four. Nothing. Five times in the river. His skin was still diseased.

He dipped for the sixth time. His skin was exactly the same as when he had started. "I hope Elisha was right," he whispered.

Naaman closed his eyes and dipped for the seventh and final time. When he came up out of the water, he could hear the shouts of his servants. Slowly he opened his eyes and looked at his arms. He was healed! All his flesh was restored. It looked like the skin of a new born baby.

Naaman went back to thank the prophet and vowed to worship the God of Israel. He returned to his own land as a missionary who fully believed in the healing power of Yahweh.

Power Points

1. God responds to faith, not to need. Jesus said, *"...there were many in Israel with leprosy in the time of Elisha the prophet, yet not one of them was cleansed-only Naaman the Syrian"* (Luke 4:27). There are millions of people who are in desperate need of healing, yet God responds to those who have faith to believe for healing. Faith is the currency of the kingdom of heaven.

2. Do not stop believing for your miracle right before it happens. Naaman was told to dip seven times. Absolutely nothing happened the first six times he dipped his body in the water. If he had stopped after the sixth dip, he would have died of leprosy. You may be doing everything you need to do to receive your healing, but you have not seen a manifestation yet. You could be on your sixth dip! Keep confessing the Word, planting seed, praying the prayer of faith, and believing God for your healing. Never give up hope. Do not stop believing right before receiving.

3. God often heals sinners as a way to bring them into His kingdom. After Naaman was healed, he began worshiping the God of Israel. Experiencing God's power is a "wake-up call" which causes many unbelievers to seek salvation.

   Why do we need miracles? One of the primary purposes of miracles is to provide a witness for unbelievers. Leonard Ravenhill said, "We do not need a new definition of the gospel, we need a new demonstration of the gospel." We need miracles because a miracle is worth a thousand sermons. There are a lot of ways to minister to people; you can feed them, love on them, and preach to them. But there is nothing like a miracle to bring a person to the Lord. Supernatural miracles prove the reality of God's existence and spark faith in unbelievers.

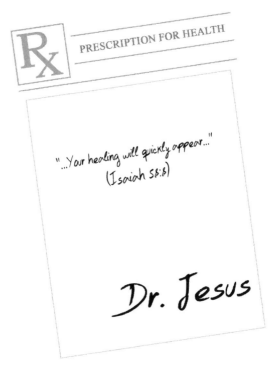

PRESCRIPTION FOR HEALTH

"...Your healing will quickly appear..."
(Isaiah 58:8)

Dr. Jesus

The Story of
the Spitting Healer

(Mark 8:22-26)

The man from Bethsaida was blind. Some of his friends took him to Jesus and begged the great healer to touch his eyes.

Jesus, ever willing to give personal attention in response to the faith of the needy, took the man by the hand and led him outside the village.

Jesus leaned close to the man's face and spit into his eyes. The man felt the wet saliva run down his face and he sensed the touch of hands on his eyes. He heard the gentle voice of Jesus asking, "Do you see anything?"

Surprised at the question, the man opened his eyelids and saw light for the first time in years. "I see people; they look like trees walking around," he told Jesus. The man had not received his full sight, but even though he was only partially healed, hope welled up inside his soul. If Jesus could make him see light, Jesus could completely heal him.

Wanting to finish what He had started, Jesus again placed His hands on the man and prayed. This time when the man opened his eyes, he could see clearly. Now people looked like people and trees looked like trees. The man who had recently been blind saw the blue sky, the green grass, and the smile on the face of Jesus. His sight was completely restored, he was healed!

Power Points
1. This man's healing was gradual. It was accomplished in stages. Some people seem to think God must always heal the sick instantaneously. But sometimes miracles take time. Be assured, *"...he who began a good work in you will carry it on to completion until the day of Christ Jesus"* (Philippians 1:6). Once God starts a miracle, He will complete it. If you have only received a partial miracle, do not get discouraged, keep believing for the full manifestation of your healing.

2. The surprising feature of this miracle is the method Jesus used to heal the man. Can you imagine being healed by someone spitting at you? Jesus was not afraid to use unorthodox means to heal this man. This tells me that Jesus is not limited to a specific method. He will use any means possible to bring healing to your body.

> **Saved in the Morning, Healed in the Afternoon**
>
> During one campaign we invited the entire city to attend our morning meetings in a local church. Since there were many Hindus scattered throughout the church crowd, I felt the need to give an opportunity to be saved.
>
> I gave the invitation, "If you want Jesus to forgive your sins, then I invite you to come to the front of the church. If you have never given your life to Jesus, then today is your day." About twenty people walked forward in response. I asked them to kneel on the ground and led them in a prayer for salvation.
>
> One of the men who came forward for salvation was crippled. He could not walk without using a cane. Joyfully, he gave his life to Jesus. Later, in the afternoon festival, the same man came to the platform. Instead of leaning on his cane, he was holding it high in the air. Jesus had healed him!

The Story of
the Woman Who Could Not
be Cured By Doctors

(Matthew 9:18-22; Mark 5:21-34; Luke 8:40-48)

S he was a desperate women. For twelve long years she had suffered from a terrible sickness. She could still remember the day the issue of blood started. At first it did not concern her, but when the bleeding continued after several days it began to worry her. Nothing she did was able to staunch the flow.

The woman went to her family doctor, but he was unable to help her. Then she found some specialists, but they were just as powerless to cure her disease. After that she bounced from doctor to doctor in an effort to find a solution. Some gave her medicine, some told her to go on vacation to rest, and some just shook their heads in resignation. There were two common denominators between the multitude of doctors: they were unable to cure her and they charged her outrageous sums of money.

Now after twelve years she was completely broke. She had spent every single penny she owned on doctors hoping they would find a cure. Her pockets were empty, and her heart was devoid of almost all hope.

One day she heard about a man named Jesus. We do not know exactly what she had heard about him, but it could have been a report about the paralytic being let down through the roof or an account about the leper being healed. Somewhere she had heard a story about Jesus healing the sick and faith sprang up within her heart.

She said to herself, "If I can just touch the edge of His clothes, I will be healed." Jesus became her last hope. She believed the reports she had heard about Him, and she was willing to step out in faith for her healing.

It was illegal for her to be in a crowd of people because her condition made her unclean. But she ignored the law and pushed her way through the crowd surrounding Jesus. Hundreds of people were around Him and she had to push, pull, and crawl through cracks in order to get near Him. Finally, she came up behind Him, reached out her hand, and touched the hem of His garment.

Immediately she felt the power of God flow through her body. The bleeding stopped and she knew her body was healed. She was healthy again!

Of course, Jesus realized that power had left His body. He had felt a sudden outpouring of power in response to the woman's faith. He turned around in the crowd and asked, "Who touched my clothes?"

The disciples thought the question was foolish. They told Him, "Master, all the people are crowding around you, how can you ask 'Who touched me?'"

The woman heard the question of Jesus and realizing what had happened to her, fell trembling at His feet with fear, and told him the whole truth. She feared His displeasure, because according to the Law (Leviticus 15:19), her touch made Him unclean until evening time. But Jesus did not condemn her; instead He completed the healing process of her soul by saying, "Daughter, your faith has healed you. Go in peace and be freed from your suffering."

Power Points
1. When you hear about Jesus, your life is about to change for the better. From the moment the woman heard about Jesus'

ability to perform miracles, she was focused on reaching Him. She knew Jesus was the answer to her problem.

2. Speaking releases faith. The woman with the issue of blood said to herself, *"If I just touch his clothes, I will be healed"* (Mark 5:21-34). This confession opened the door for her to receive her miracle.

3. The woman believed the reports she heard about Jesus. This belief literally created her miracle. Jesus explained, *"Daughter, your faith has healed you"* (Mark 5:34). Believing is the catalyst that turns God's promises into God's power. Every Biblical promise contains the power necessary to make it come to pass, if only someone will believe and act upon that belief.

4. The woman took action by pushing through the crowd until she could touch the hem of Christ's garment. Faith is never static, it always takes action. Begin using your faith right now and take action. Do something you were not able to do before. If you have not been able to stand up before, try to stand up now. If you have not been able to use your arm in a certain way, begin moving it now. Whatever you were unable to do before, use your faith and start doing it.

5. Marilyn Hickey believes dis-ease is the exact opposite of being at ease. When Jesus healed the woman with the issue of blood, He said "Go in peace." For the first time in twelve years she was at ease. What a peaceful feeling it must have been to be completely free from disease. Jesus takes dis-ease and turns it into perfect ease.

God is ready right now to heal you. God is a God of the now. He does not want to wait until tomorrow, or the next day, *"now is the time of God's favor, now is the day of salvation"* (2 Corinthians 6:2). Now is the time for your salvation from sickness.

6. After she was healed, the woman testified to Jesus about her healing. After we are healed, we need to testify by telling people about our healing. Our testifying produces faith in others so the circle of miracles can continue.

The Story of
the Four Faith-Filled Friends

(Matthew 9:1-8; Mark 2:1-12; Luke 5:17-26).

When Jesus went to the town of Capernaum, news of His arrival quickly spread. Hundreds flocked to the house where He was staying until there was no room left inside. The latecomers pushed close until even the door of the house was completely blocked. The faith of this crowd was strong and the power of the Lord was present to heal.

After Jesus began teaching, four men arrived carrying a friend who was completely paralyzed. They tried to push their way through the crowd, but the people were bunched together too closely for them to get through. Suddenly, one of the men had an idea, "Let's take him up onto the roof."

They carried the man to the roof and began tearing a hole in the tiles. We do not know whose house this was, but since Peter lived in the town of Capernaum, it could have been his house. I wonder what the owner thought when he felt pieces of the roof falling on his head. After the hole was big enough, the men lowered their friend through the tiles into the middle of the crowd, right in front of Jesus.

When Jesus saw their faith, He said "Friend, your sins are forgiven." That day there were many Pharisees and teachers of the law who were listening to Jesus. When they heard Jesus forgive the man's sins they began thinking to themselves, "Who is this fellow who speaks blasphemy? Who can forgive sins but God alone?"

Of course Jesus was God, and He knew what they were thinking. He asked them, "Why are you thinking these things in your hearts? Which is easier: to say, 'Your sins are forgiven,' or to say, 'Get up and walk'? But that you may know that the Son of Man has authority on earth to forgive sins..." He turned to the paralyzed man, "...I tell you, get up, take your mat and go home."

Immediately the paralyzed man stood up in front of them, took what he had been lying on and went home triumphantly carrying his mat and praising God.

The crowd was amazed and gave praise to God. Everyone was filled with awe and whispered to each other, "We have seen remarkable things today."

Power Points

1. Jesus healed this man because of the faith of his friends. Gordon Lindsay writes, "Jesus showed that it is possible for others to supply the needed faith when the sick person is unable to supply it for himself." If you have a friend who is sick, your faith can help bring healing!

2. Uncommon faith produces uncommon results. When the men found it impossible to push through the crowd, they discovered an unorthodox solution to their problem. They were persistent until their friend was healed. After they showed such great faith, how could Jesus not heal the paralyzed man?

3. Forgiving sins and healing are tied together. The Pharisees doubted Jesus' ability to forgive sins because only God can forgive sins. But only God could have healed the man. If Jesus can do something only God can do by healing the man,

does this not prove that He can also forgive sins, another action only God can do? This double miracle demonstrates that both healing and forgiveness of sins are included in the ministry of Jesus Christ.

The Story of
Blind Bartimaeus

(Matthew 20:29-34; Mark 10:46-52; Luke 18:35-43)

B artimaeus was sitting beside the road begging. The sun was shining, the birds were flying, and the dusty road stretched back towards Jericho. But Bartimaeus could see none of this because he was blind.

Off in the distance Bartimaeus heard a crowd coming. When they drew closer, he cried out to the nearest passer-by, "What's happening?"

"Everyone's out here to see Jesus of Nazareth," the reply came.

As soon as Bartimaeus heard who it was, he began to shout, "Jesus, Son of David, have mercy on me!"

Again and again he shouted until the people near him told him to be quiet, yet he continued to shout as loud as he could, "Jesus, Son of David, have mercy on me!"

Suddenly Jesus stopped walking. He had heard the desperate plea for help. Jesus looked around and seeing the blind man, He called out to him, "Come."

The same people who had been commanding Bartimaeus to be quiet moments before now told him, "Cheer up! Get on your feet. Jesus is calling for you."

Bartimaeus threw his cloak aside, jumped to his feet and came to Jesus.

"What do you want me to do for you?" Jesus asked.

"Teacher, I want to see" the blind man replied.

"Go, your faith has healed you," Jesus said. Immediately, blind Bartimaeus was no longer blind. He could see!

Power Points

1. Where did Bartimaeus hear about Jesus' ability to heal blind people? In Luke 18:35-43, we find a story about a blind man who Jesus healed when going into Jericho. The story about Bartimaeus happens when Jesus is leaving Jericho. In all other details, both stories are very similar. Some scholars think both stories are about the same miracle and that the Gospel writers were confused about whether Jesus was coming or going.

But I think the Gospel writers were both correct. I believe the day before Jesus healed Bartimaeus, He healed another blind man as He entered Jericho. This man who was healed returned to the beggar's colony and told everyone about his healing. The next day when Bartimaeus heard Jesus was passing by, he knew it was his opportunity for a miracle.

Bartimaeus received his miracle because his faith had been built up by the other man's testimony. This shows

> **Hoping for Money, Woman Receives Miracle**
>
> At our festival in Panama, one crippled woman hobbled onto the field with a scheme to make some money. She brought her own offering bag. When we took up the offering, she pretended to be an usher and passed her bag around. Then she stuffed the bag filled with bills and coins under her shirt. One of the ushers saw her steal and reported her to a nearby policeman. He came and took the offering bag away from her and made her sit behind the platform. When we began praying for the sick, Jesus touched her and she started walking without using her crutches. She came up to the platform and testified that she arrived looking for money, but instead she received a miracle.

us how important it is for us to share our testimony with others.

2. Jesus asked Bartimaeus a question, "What do you want me to do for you?" Now Bartimaeus could have asked for some money, or an autograph, or a touch from the hand of Jesus, but the blind man knew exactly what he wanted. He said, "Teacher, I want to see."

   In response Jesus gave him what he asked for. This means we need to be specific in our prayer requests. Tell God precisely what you desire. You will receive exactly what you believe for.

3. When Bartimaeus stood up to go to Jesus, he threw his coat aside. Why is this important? Well, in those days, beggars wore a special color of cloak which identified them as professional beggars. When others saw that type of cloak, they would throw money. By leaving his cloak behind, Bartimaeus was abandoning his livelihood. He was blind and the crowd was huge; there was no way he was going to find his cloak again. He had such complete faith that Jesus was going to heal him that he knew he would never need his begging cloak again.

   I heard a joke about a man who fell off the edge of a cliff and was hanging by his fingertips from a rock hundreds of feet above the hard ground below. He began crying for help when suddenly he heard a voice say, "This is God. What can I do for you?"

   "What a relief," he exclaimed, "Please, reach your mighty hand down here, pick me up, and place me back on top of the cliff."

   In reply, God said, "Let go of the rock you are hanging onto and I will catch you."

The man thought about it for a moment, then yelled towards the top of the cliff, "Is there anyone else up there?" The man was not willing to put his complete faith in God.

Just as Bartimaeus left his cloak behind, we should let go of our past and trust God for our future. Leave your cloak behind; burn your bridges; drop the crutch of yesterday's failures; let go of your rope and put all your faith in God's ability to catch you.

4. The crowd told Bartimaeus to be quiet but he continued to call out to Jesus. Even when others are telling you to give up hope, keep crying out persistently until you receive an answer from Jesus.

Questions...

God desires for His children to walk in health. Unfortunately, there is a lot of sickness in the world.

What causes sickness?

Why do people get sick? There are three causes of sickness. Disease can be attributed to living in a sinful world because of the fall of Adam and Eve, to the work of Satan, and to natural causes. Let's examine each of these.

1. Sin causes disease

When God created the earth, He did not create sickness. He made the birds of the air, the fish of the sea, the plants, and the animals, but He did not create cold viruses or cancers. These appeared when Satan corrupted God's perfect plan.

God commanded Adam and Eve, *"You are free to eat from any tree in the garden; but you must not eat from the tree of the knowledge of good and evil, for when you eat of it you will surely die"* (Genesis 2:16-17).

One day, Eve was walking in the Garden of Eden when she heard a voice. Up until that moment, she had only heard the voices of Adam and God so this new sound intrigued her. She looked around until she spotted a serpent wrapped around a branch of the forbidden tree.

The serpent hissed, "Did God really say, 'You must not eat from any tree in the garden?'"

"We may eat fruit from the trees in the garden, but God did say, 'You must not eat fruit from the tree that is in the middle of the garden, and you must not touch it, or you will die,'" Eve helpfully explained.

"You will not surely die," the serpent said, flatly contradicting God Almighty. "For God knows that when you eat of it your eyes will be opened, and you will be like God, knowing good and evil." By saying this, the devil was tempting her to question God's word.

When Eve heard this lie, she looked at the fruit and she saw it was pleasing to the eye and good for food. In direct disobedience to her Creator, she reached out her hand, plucked a piece of fruit from the tree, and took a bite. She handed some fruit to her husband, and he took a bite, too.

At that moment sickness entered the world. Eve began to die a slow but inevitable death. Immediately her belly began to ache as she realized what she had done. This was a new sensation; none of the other food in the garden had caused her to want to throw up. Adam experienced the first headache as he frantically tried to think of a way to undo the great wrong.

Because of their high treason, Adam and Eve died spiritually, and began to die physically. Their organs began to wear out and entropy started to cause sickness in their bodies. Adam would live another nine hundred and thirty years, but his death was set in motion that day. As James 1:15 explains, "...*Sin, when it is full-grown, gives birth to death.*"

Sickness is the result of sin. It stems from a breaking of fellowship with God. The root cause of sickness is the original sin of Satan when he rebelled against God. This sickness spread to earth when Adam and Eve disobeyed God in the Garden of Eden. Ultimately all sickness can be traced back to sin.

Since sickness is caused by sin, humanity is in desperate need of salvation from both sin and from the effects of sin. Sin is a dirty stain upon the wonder of God's creation. Because of the fall, creation was corrupted. What God intended for good, the devil turned into evil.

Sin, death, and sickness entered the world because of Adam's disobedience. Paul explains the connection between sin and death, *"...just as sin entered the world through one man, and death through sin, and in this way death came to all men, because all sinned"* (Romans 5:12). Death (and sickness which leads to death) came into the world because of Adam, and in this way, death (sickness) came to the entire human race, because all have sinned.

Sickness is not necessarily the result of an individual's specific sin, rather, it is caused by living in a sinful, imperfect world. During the time of Jesus, Jewish culture believed that all sickness could be traced back to a specific sin. Jesus shattered this misconception when his disciples asked him about a blind man, "Teacher, who sinned, this man or his parents, that he was born blind?"

"Neither this man nor his parents sinned," replied Jesus (see John 9).

The man's blindness was simply the result of living in a sinful world. Jesus proceeded to spit on the ground, formed mud from his saliva, wiped the mud on the man's eyes, and told him to go wash in a pool. When the man obeyed Jesus, he was completely healed. Jesus cured the man so that the work of God might be displayed in his life.

Jesus denied this man's blindness was caused by a specific sin. But at another time, Jesus did not deny the possibility that a specific sin could cause a disease. Earlier Jesus had found another man he had healed in the temple and said to him, *"...you are well again. Stop sinning or something worse may happen to you"* (See John 5:1-15).

By saying this Jesus acknowledged the possibility that sin can lead to sickness. For example, most sexual diseases would not be a problem if every man and woman stayed married in a monogamous marriage as God intended. Sexual sin often leads to sexual disease. In the same way, there are other diseases which are caused by specific sins.

Sin separates us from God's healing power. It is a roadblock between our prayers and God. *"But your iniquities have separated you from your God; your sins have hidden his face from you, so that he will not hear"* (Isaiah 59:2).

The good news is that repentance brings healing for diseases related to specific sins and for sicknesses caused by the general sinfulness of the world. *"Therefore confess your sins to each other and pray for each other so that you may be healed..."* (James 5:16). If sin has caused sickness in your life, simply repent of every sin and pray for your healing. God wants to forgive our sins and heal our diseases (Psalm 103:3). He will completely forgive you and from His forgiveness will flow healing power.

The confession of sins opens the door for God to move. When you confess your sins, it breaks the power of sin over your life. By asking forgiveness you invite God to remove all the effects of sin, including sickness, from your life.

2. The work of Satan causes disease

"The thief comes only to steal and kill and destroy..." (John 10:10). Satan wants to steal your health, kill your body, and destroy your life. The devil is the author of disease and he purposely invented the cruelest, most inhumane sickness he could imagine to help him accomplish his evil schemes.

Jesus definitely attributed sickness to Satan. In fact, he used precisely the same cutting word, *"epitimao,"* to rebuke both demons (Luke 4:35) and sickness (Luke 4:39). Jesus knew both came from the same place, the pits of hell.

Some diseases are directly caused by demonic possession. One day a crowd brought Jesus a demon-possessed man who was both

97

blind and mute. Jesus threw out the demon and completely healed him so he could both talk and see (Matthew 12:22).

The last time I cleaned out my refrigerator, I discovered a dish of food on the bottom shelf right at the back. It had been there so long that I was not able to remember what it was so I cracked open the lid. Immediately an awful stench filled the room. The food was rotten. As soon as I smelled the bad food, I threw it away. Then I took the trash bag out of the trash can and tossed it outside. The entire time I had a look of disgusted revulsion on my face. This is how Jesus must have felt when He threw out demons. When something smells bad, you do not tolerate its presence.

Not every sickness is a direct result of a demon, but in the Bible we do see Satan's forces causing fevers, muteness, deafness, blindness, and even epilepsy. The good news is that Jesus came to destroy, ruin, and demolish the works of the devil. *"...the reason the Son of God appeared was to destroy the devil's work"* (1 John 3:8).

When the Gospel writers told about Jesus casting out demons, they used the word *ekballo* to describe the process. This is a compound word made up of the word *ek* meaning "out" and *ballo* meaning "to throw" (*ballo* is where we get the word "ball"). When these two words are combined, they mean "to throw out" or "to violently cast out." Jesus violently threw out the demons.

When I think of Jesus "throwing out" demons, I imagine a baseball game with Jesus as the pitcher. Every time a demon steps up to home plate hoping to hit the ball out of the ballpark, I see Jesus throwing the demon out. One strike, two strikes, three strikes, and the demon is out of there!

When he goes back to his bench, the demon complains to the devil, "Coach, we're never going to win this ball game, that guy pitches way too fast."

Satan glares at the demon, "Don't make excuses. I hit the ball once, and it went a long, long way."

The demon mumbles under his breath, "Yeah, you thought you had a home run, but on the third day, His Father caught the ball, and you were out permanently."

In that great game, Jesus defeated every demonic power and authority and made a public spectacle of them as He triumphed over them at the cross (Colossians 2:15). When Jesus left for heaven, He called in his twelve relief pitchers and gave them the secret to His pitching record. Now every believer has the ability to cast out demons the same way Jesus did! He said, *"...In my name they will drive out demons..."* (Mark 16:17).

Satan has been defeated, his power is destroyed, and Jesus has won the ball game! Now all we need to do is remind the devil of the score.

3. Neglect of natural law causes disease

When I was a child, I loved playing outside in the rain. It was so much fun to splash in the puddles and to feel the raindrops hitting my face. However, without fail, my wise mother would call me inside once she saw the rain. When I complained, she would carefully explain, "Daniel, while it might be fun to play in the rain, it is not advisable to be outside in the rain. Why? Because kids who get chilly and wet often catch colds."

There are certain, unchangeable laws of nature which must be followed in order to maintain a healthy body. Some people whine, "The devil is attacking me with this awful disease," but in reality, Satan had nothing to do with them getting sick. Their infirmity is a direct result of their own lack of wisdom. They caught a cold because they played in the rain; they have cancer because they smoked; their feet are sore because they are overweight from eating too much junk food; or they are afflicted with a heart disease because of a lack of exercise.

When Satan told Jesus to jump off the roof of the temple, Jesus told him, "Thou shalt not tempt the Lord your God." Jesus knew there are certain natural laws which should not be disobeyed. There is a law which states, "Thou shalt not fall from high places lest thou be smashed," just as there is an unstated law which says, "Thou shalt not continually eat junk food lest thou become overweight and prone to heart disease." Do not tempt God by disobeying natural law.

In many of these cases, God does not instantly heal the illness, because an instant healing would only be a temporary solution. The sickness is actually a symptom of a greater problem. In order to obtain true healing, we need to change the habits which led to the disease. The good news is that God will give us wisdom on how to undo the harm caused by our own foolishness. With His help we can achieve complete healing!

Your body is the temple of the Holy Spirit (1 Corinthians 6:19). God wants you to keep the inside of the temple clean and the outside of the temple in good shape.

Does God Cause Sickness?

Does God cause sickness? No! It is completely against His nature. Everything that is good comes from God and everything that is bad comes from the devil. Sickness is undeniably bad.

Norvel Hays says, "No sickness or disease comes from heaven because none can be found there." If God wanted to put sickness on someone, He would have to borrow it from the devil. This is such a ridiculous picture, can you imagine God going to Satan and saying, "Listen, there is this guy I need to teach a lesson, can I borrow a little bit of cancer?"

I think God is perfectly capable of teaching me without making me sick. There are other ways to get my attention. On the cross, Jesus bore our sicknesses on His own body. After paying such a high price to get rid of pain, why would He choose to put that pain on someone?

Jesus said, *"...the Son of Man did not come to destroy men's lives, but to save them"* (Luke 9:56). Jesus comes to save your life, not to take it from you. Not once did Jesus make anyone sick during His ministry here on earth. If Jesus had wanted to use sickness to punish someone, all the Pharisees of his day would have died from leprosy. But Jesus always responds in love to those who oppose Him. It is completely against His nature to make a person sick.

In Mexico they have a saying, "The apple does not fall far from the tree," meaning that sons are often like their fathers. Well, I want to tell you, Jesus is exactly the same as His Father (Hebrews 1:3). If Jesus did not make people sick when He was on earth, his Father will not make people sick today.

Have you ever been to a pool and seen the round styrofoam rings hanging near the water? These are strategically placed so the lifeguards can throw them to a swimmer who is in trouble. When someone is drowning, those rings can save a life! Jesus is like the life-saver thrown to a drowning person; He does not pull you down, He lifts you up. Our Lord is a Life-Savior.

Can you imagine the uproar if a lifeguard saw a drowning child and started throwing bricks instead of the life-saving device? Unfortunately, some churches are throwing drowning people bricks of doubt like: "God does not heal anymore," or "God is using sickness to teach you a lesson." These words of doubt will take a drowning man straight to the bottom of the ocean.

Always remember, Jesus will never pull you down, He will always lift you up. Christ does not take your life, He saves your life. The Son of God will never make you sick; He will always make you well.

God is on your side, He wants to heal you. God is not looking for a way to bring you home to heaven, He wants you to live a full, satisfying, healthy life right here on earth. Oral Roberts once said, "I believe in healing because I believe in Jesus Christ." Jesus and healing are inseparable because healing is an essential component of Christ's nature.

Did God cause Job's Sickness?

I am extremely surprised that anyone would blame Job's sickness on God. The Bible clearly says Satan caused Job's troubles, *"... Satan went out from the presence of the LORD and afflicted Job with painful sores from the soles of his feet to the top of his head"* (Job 2:7). Do not attribute the work of Satan to God.

The reason people say God put sickness on Job is because God allowed it to happen. Now, in a sense, this is true. Nothing can occur without God permitting it. But since God has given His creation free choice, many bad events happen which God does not want to happen. God permits them to take place, but He does not cause them.

Hindus Discover Jesus is Alive

In Surkhet, Nepal, the first night's message was on the power of the Name of Jesus. Thousands of people shouted the Name of Jesus, many of them Hindus calling on Jesus for the first time.

In the middle of the sermon, an elderly gentleman to the right of the platform jumped to his feet and lifted his walking cane in the air. He started to shout, "I'm healed! I'm healed!" The entire crowd turned to look at him. He threw his cane to the ground and began lifting his hands over his head. There was a huge smile on his wrinkled face. After this spontaneous miracle, the preaching ended abruptly as God began to touch people across the field.

People streamed forward to give their testimonies. A blind eye was opened. A man with back pain for four years was healed. Then, a Hindu man came to the platform. He explained that he had been deaf in his right ear for five years. As he listened to the sermon, his ear popped open and he was able to hear. We tested his hearing and he was able to repeat even the softest whisper.

At the end of the first day's service as people left the field, it was obvious that word about what had happened was going to spread across the city. Because of the miracles, thousands of Hindus turned their back on three hundred and thirty million gods in order to follow the one true God, Jesus Christ.

Repeatedly, Satan asked God to stretch out His hand against Job. Because of Satan's words, some Christians think God put sickness on Job, but consider the source. It is Satan speaking. I think Satan was mocking God by asking Him to do something which God would obviously never do.

Even though God gave Satan permission to put sickness on Job, God did not commission him to make Job sick. As Kenneth Hagan explained, "God will permit you to rob a gas station, but he won't commission you to do it."

In reality God simply allowed the devil to operate based on the principles of free choice. Satan tried to pin the blame on God; Job's friends blamed God, and even Job suspected God caused his sickness, but God never claims responsibility. The Bible wholly places the blame for Job's troubles on Satan.

At the end of the book of Job, we see God's true character. He enters the scene as a healer who restores Job's health and wealth. God is always a healer, never a destroyer.

What was Paul's Thorn in the Flesh?

Was the thorn in Paul's flesh a literal sickness? Some scholars believe the thorn Paul mentions in 2 Corinthians 12:7, was an eye disease. This conclusion is based on circumstantial evidence found in Galatians 4, Paul reminds the Galatians *"it was because of an illness that I first preached the gospel to you."* Two verses later, he says *"if you could have done so, you would have torn out your eyes and given them to me."* The close proximity of the mention of an illness and the mention of his eyes suggests that his illness could have been in his eyes. Later in the same letter, Paul says, *"See what large letters I use as I write to you with my own hand!"* (Galatians 6:11). If Paul did have problems with his eyes, he would have written big letters. However, all this evidence is nothing but guesswork.

Paul never actually says the thorn is a sickness. In fact, he calls it "a messenger from Satan." The Greek word for messenger is *angelos* which is found in the New Testament over one hundred times. The word is translated "messenger" a total of seven times, but not once is it used to mean "sickness." Nowhere else in the Bible is a sickness called a "messenger from Satan." In Numbers 33:55, the inhabitants of the land of Canaan are called "thorns in your sides," and in Joshua 23:13 the inhabitants of Canaan are called "thorns in your eyes." In both these cases, "thorns" are personalities. I think this "thorn" was a demon or a person who plagued Paul. Therefore, there is no reason to suppose Paul's thorn was a sickness.

Does God want You to Live a Life of Wholeness?

Sickness is a spiritual, mental, or physical lack of wholeness. People are three part beings composed of a spirit, a soul, and a body. At our innermost core, we are spirit beings. We have a soul made up of the mind, the will, and the emotions. We live in a body. A lack of wholeness in any one of these areas can produce a visible manifestation of physical sickness. For example, the body needs certain vitamins and minerals in order to operate at peek efficiency. If the body does not get its whole quota of vitamins, eventually the body will deteriorate and get sick. A lack of wholeness in the body produces physical symptoms.

A lack of wholeness in the soul can also cause sickness. Emotional stress and mental disease often leads to physical sickness. Illness can also be caused by a poor mental attitude. Science has demonstrated that many people are sick because they think they are sick. This stems from a lack of mental wholeness.

Another serious cause of disease is a lack of wholeness in the spirit. Sin, even a small sin, creates a downward spiral which ultimately ends in death. Sin is a sickness of the spirit which causes physical ailments.

The goal of Jesus is to restore wholeness to the whole man. When Jesus healed the paralyzed man who was let down through the roof by his friends, He cured three problems. First, He encouraged the man's soul by saying, "Take heart" or "Be of good cheer." Second, He cured the man's spiritual condition by forgiving his sins. Third, He healed the man's physical body. This restored the man to full mental, physical, and spiritual health.

God wants you to experience more than a one-time physical healing, He wants you to walk in divine health: spirit, soul, and body. Healing is more than an event, it is a process. In the case of this man who was let down through the roof, Jesus only restored the man's physical health after He had restored his mental and spiritual health.

Jesus wants to restore people to a state of complete wholeness. It is useless for God to heal your body if your spirit is broken or your emotional makeup is unstable. Jesus will always do what is necessary to make you whole.

Why Do Some People Lose Their Healing?

Jesus told this story, *"When an evil spirit comes out of a man, it goes through arid places seeking rest and does not find it. Then it says, 'I will return to the house I left.' When it arrives, it finds the house unoccupied, swept clean and put in order. Then it goes and takes with it seven other spirits more wicked than itself, and they go in and live there. And the final condition of that man is worse than the first..."* (Matthew 12:43-45).

The demons who caused your sickness have grown comfortable playing havoc with your body. After disease is cast out of your body, demonic powers will often try to return with a stronger attack. You must maintain your healing by living in an atmosphere of faith. Beat off this "second wave" attack by continuing to speak words of faith over your life. Stand firm; resist the devil; and claim your healing.

In order to maintain your healing, you need to stay in constant contact with your Healer. Notice that the demon in Jesus' illustration returns to find the house "unoccupied." You can only resist the re-entry of the devil if you keep your life filled with God. Do not leave a "Vacancy" sign on the door of your heart. Remember, if Satan can find a place inside you, he will take it.

Satan will often attempt to steal our healing by redoubling his efforts to tempt us. Jesus said to one man who was healed, *"...you are well again. Stop sinning or something worse may happen to you"* (John 5:14). If you begin to sin after being healed, it opens the door for the devil to attack your life again. In order to keep your healing, it is vital to be filled with the Holy Spirit and to resist temptation.

You can also claim God's promise found in Nahum 1:9, *"affliction shall not rise up the second time"* (KJV). It is never God's will for you to become sick again. If Satan tries to put the same old sickness on you by reminding you of your past, just remind him of his future!

Why Do Some Healings Take a Long Time?

John Tasch told me this story. In China there is a type of bamboo which achieves spectacular growth in a very short period of time. This Chinese bamboo will actually grow to the height of a nine story building. However, it requires careful planning to prepare for the growth. The gardener must plant the seed in perfect soil, then he must faithfully water the seed.

For the entire first year that the gardener waters the plant, nothing happens. Even though the plant can not be seen, the gardener must continue to water and fertilize the soil. Two years pass, nothing has happened. Three years, and the gardener must still water the plant. Four years go by and still there is not one sign of the bamboo above the surface of the dirt. Finally, in the fifth year a tiny shoot appears.

Within five weeks from the time the first leaf appears, the bamboo will grow to a height of over ninety feet tall! Did that bamboo grow ninety feet tall in five weeks, or did it grow ninety feet tall in five years?

Even though amazing growth could be seen over a five week period, it actually took five years for the Chinese bamboo to grow. If the gardener had taken even a month off from watering the ground where the bamboo seed was planted, the growth spurt would never have happened. For five years, the plant was putting roots down into the ground so it could support its dramatic growth. Without five years of watering, five weeks of growth could never happen.

Our faith often works the same way. For years, we develop our faith by reading God's Word, by confessing His promises, and by praying. Then, when we need a miracle, it can happen instantaneously. But did that miracle really happen in an instant, or did it require us to build up our faith for years beforehand?

This is why it is so important for you to read this book, even if you are not sick. Right now you are building your faith for healing, so when Satan tries to attack you, you will be ready for an instant miracle.

If you are sick, you need to continue building your faith. Keep reading God's Word and confessing His promises. Your healing shall surely come! Even if you do not see any evidence of your healing right now, keep watering your faith. It is planting deep roots into your heart, and when the time is perfect, God will perform a spectacular miracle!

Why are Some Not Healed?
1. Ignorance of God's promises

The number one reason people are not healed is because they are ignorant of God's promises concerning healing. God says, *"my people are destroyed from lack of knowledge..."* (Hosea 4:6). This is one of the greatest tragedies in the church today.

Knowledge is the only antidote for ignorance. God proclaims, "I am the Lord your healer;" the Gospels are full of stories about Jesus healing people; and the Bible has hundreds of promises concerning healing. We can cure our ignorance by becoming familiar with the truth of God's Word.

Daniel King

When I took tests in college, I read the textbook, took detailed notes, and repeated the material over and over again until I thoroughly grasped it. This same process is great for building faith for healing. Read the Bible, take notes on what it says about healing, and verbally repeat the truths over and over again (this is called confession) until you absolutely know God's will concerning healing.

2. Traditions of man

Over the centuries, man has invented traditions which are not found in the Bible. Some churches say the age of miracles is past, others say God makes people sick in order to teach them a lesson, still others say it is not God's will to heal. How did these traditions develop?

The early church believed in healing and regularly experienced great healing miracles. But over time, as some church members grew lukewarm, there was not enough faith to believe for healing. Rather than blaming this absence of healing on their own missing faith, man invented reasons to blame the lack of healing on God. Because they did not experience miracles, they did not believe miracles were possible.

Never allow a negative experience determine your theology. Most doctrines of healing are based on man's experience (or lack of experience), rather than on God's Word. Do not permit someone's past failures to dictate your level of trust in God. Why should you accept the word of a preacher or scholar who has a doubt based theology? Doubt and unbelief are not gospel truth, instead they are a perverse lie about the good news.

Your theology should be based on God's Word. If you can not take His words as absolute truth, what right do you have believing you are saved? If one accepts the fact that God wants to save us, one must also accept the indisputable fact that God wants us to walk in divine health. Neither the doctrine of salvation nor the doctrine of

108

healing are based on experience, rather, they are based on faith in God's Word.

How do you know you are going to heaven when you die? Did you ever die and go to heaven? No, you know you are saved because of your faith in God's promises concerning salvation.

How do you know you are going to be healed? It does not matter whether you have a physical manifestation of healing yet. You can know you will be healed because of your faith in God's promises concerning healing. You were healed two thousand years ago; you are healed right now, and you will be healed.

3. Sin

Sin stops God's blessings. When we deliberately hide sin in our hearts, our prayers bounce off the gates of heaven. As the psalmist pointed out, *"If I had cherished sin in my heart, the Lord would not have listened"* (Psalm 66:18). Entering the throne room of God begins with repentance.

There are two sins which are particularly dangerous. First, unforgiveness towards another human creates a bitter acid which eats away at your spiritual man. Eventually this will affect your physical body. Unforgiveness in your heart hurts you far more than it hurts the person it is directed towards. If you are angry at someone, repent and forgive and this will open the door for your healing.

Second, it is important not to get bitter. All too often people say, "Well, I prayed for my aunt for three years and she died of cancer. I don't believe in that healing stuff." Their bitterness is cutting off the flow of God's blessing. If you are bitter towards God, repentance is the key to your healing. Do not allow yesterday's failures to prevent you from receiving today's miracle.

The good news is the blood of Jesus washes away every sin the moment you repent and ask forgiveness. Once the dirty stains of sin are replaced with clean robes of righteousness, God is able to move in the area of healing.

4. Lack of Faith

When Jesus visited His hometown of Nazareth, He was powerless to heal because of their unbelief. *"Coming to his hometown, he began teaching the people in their synagogue, and they were amazed. 'Where did this man get this wisdom and these miraculous powers?' they asked. 'Isn't this the carpenter's son? Isn't his mother's name Mary, and aren't his brothers James, Joseph, Simon and Judas? Aren't all his sisters with us? Where then did this man get all these things?' And they took offense at him. But Jesus said to them, 'Only in his hometown and in his own house is a prophet without honor.' And he did not do many miracles there because of their lack of faith"* (Matthew 13:54-58). In this case, healing power ceased when unbelief started.

Your spiritual life is like a teeter-totter. God is on one side casting a vote in your favor, and Satan is on the other side casting a vote against you. The direction you walk determines which way the teeter totters. God is for you, Satan is against you, and your faith is the determining factor in what happens to you.

5. Divine Mystery

A lack of faith is not the only reason some are not healed. There are some faithful Christians who do many of the right things and still die. Oral Roberts was once asked why some are not healed. He answered, "I don't know why some are healed and some are not, but I thank God for those who are healed."

Because God is omnipresent, He hears every prayer. Because God is omnipotent, He has the power to answer every prayer. But because God is omniscient, He does not always answer prayers in the way we want Him to. Since our Father is all-knowing, He knows what is best for His children. Sometimes when God's children ask for healing, they are not healed immediately, but this does not mean God will not heal them.

In the Chronicles of Narnia, C.S. Lewis uses a lion named Aslan to represent Jesus. One of Lewis' characters observes that this lion is a safe lion, but not a tame one. He will not hurt anyone, but he cannot be ordered around either. There is an old joke which children tell which asks, "Where does a lion sit in the park?" The answer? "Anywhere he wants to." God, like the king of the beasts, is sovereign. One is absolutely safe in His hands, but one can not force Him to do anything He is not ready to do.

Paul writes, *"Oh, the depth of the riches of the wisdom and knowledge of God! How unsearchable his judgments, and his paths beyond tracing out! "Who has known the mind of the Lord? Or who has been his counselor? Who has ever given to God, that God should repay him? For from him and through him and to him are all things. To him be the glory forever! Amen"* (Romans 11:33-36).

At times the mystery of why some are not healed must be left in God's hands. I do know we should not allow failures to reduce our faith in God's ability to heal. Divine mystery must be left a mystery, but there is one thing that must not remain a mystery. God wants all His children to walk in supernatural health, and eventually all believers will be resurrected with bodies which will not decay or perish. On that day sickness will be a thing of the past!

Can I have Faith in God and still Go to Doctors?

Health care is one of this nation's largest industries. The quest for health consumes almost twelve percent of our gross national product and employs millions of health care professionals. It is undeniable that thousands of people are healed by the medical profession each year. Medicines, surgery, and therapy are all used by God to heal.

I appreciate the medical world, but I believe every cure is wrought by God whether the cure comes through medical means or supernatural intervention. C.S. Lewis says, "All who are cured are cured by [God], not merely in the sense that His providence provides them with medical assistance and wholesome environments, but also in the sense that their very tissues are repaired by the far-descended energy which, flowing from Him, energizes the whole system of Nature."

Each of us is *"fearfully and wonderfully made"* (Psalm 139:14), and the entire healing process is dependant upon the principles of healing which God built into the amazingly resilient human body. All healing can ultimately be traced back to God; He created the plants from which medicines come; He created the brains of the surgeons, and He guides their hands as they operate. God is the healer regardless of whether medicine or doctors help bring healing. We should always give God credit for our healing and thank Him for the skill of the doctors treating us.

I do not believe it is right to trust God for healing while ignoring the medical profession. In fact, every medicine is against disease, which is more than I can say about every Christian. Since all healing comes from God, it is fine to seek help from medical science. You can trust God for protection when you are driving, but at the same time it is prudent to wear a seatbelt. In the same way, you can believe in "faith healing" and still go to doctors without compromising your faith.

Doctors deserve a lot of credit, but they do not have all the answers either. For example, the woman with the issue of blood visited doctors for twelve long years. She spent all of her money on physicians, but they were unable to help her. When doctors give up, it is time for Dr. Jesus to take over!

Jesus is the Great Physician. He specializes in every disease. He never makes a wrong diagnosis. He never prescribes the wrong medicine. He never does invasive surgery. At no time do you have to worry about germs after He touches you. You never have to wait in long lines to see Him. You do not have to fill out paperwork on your medical history because He already knows your medical history more intimately than you do. He does every surgery for free so you do not have to worry about whether your HMO will cover His bill. His office is open twenty-four hours a day, seven days a week, fifty-two weeks a year. Dr. Jesus is definitely the best choice for medical help.

Does Sickness have to be a part of Dying?

God did not promise us we would never die (Hebrews 9:27), but He did assure the Israelites, *"Worship the LORD your God, and...I will take away sickness from among you and...I will give you a full life span"* (Exodus 23:25-26). According to this verse, if you will worship God and obey His Word, He has guaranteed you a healthy body until your life

Half-Blind Policeman Can Now See

"You need more security," the police chief in Faisalabad, Pakistan told us. We suspected that the main reason he wanted us to have more security was because he wanted us to pay his policemen overtime. He sent over two hundred police to protect us.

One of the policemen was named Mohammad Nasim. He was blind in his left eye because of a training accident. One night, Jesus healed his eye and suddenly, he was able to see. The Muslim policeman came to the platform and told the entire crowd that Jesus had healed him. Because of this miracle, all the policemen started bringing their wives and children to the festival so that they could see what Jesus was doing.

span is complete. There is a set number of years you are predestined to live in order to fulfill God's plan for your life. If you die before your designated time, your work is cut short. And if you are hindered by sickness, it is impossible to fully achieve your mission.

I believe God wants us to die without ever being sick. I want to live my life to the fullest, and when it is time for me to go to heaven, I want to simply fall asleep and never wake up again. God does not want us to die after a long, painful disease; He wants us to live in peace until the day we are called home.

Can I Heal the Sick?

Every day Jesus healed as many sick people as He could. He traveled from village to village preaching the good news, building faith inside His listeners, and healing their diseases. But, Jesus realized it was physically impossible for Him to heal every single sick person in Israel.

One day He was looking out over the massive crowds and He had compassion on them. The people looked like rolling waves of grain, a huge harvest field ready to be harvested for the kingdom of God. Jesus knew He would be unable to bring in this mighty harvest all by Himself so He told the disciples to pray that the Lord of the harvest would send forth laborers into the harvest fields.

Now the Bible does not tell us if the disciples obeyed Jesus and prayed for laborers to go into the harvest fields, but I think they did because in the very next verse the prayer is answered. Jesus sends the disciples out as laborers into the world's harvest fields. This is exciting because the disciples became the answer to their own prayers!

Let's look at what Jesus did, *"He called his twelve disciples to him and gave them authority to drive out evil spirits and to heal every disease and sickness"* (Matthew 10:1). Wow! Just a few verses before, the Bible tells us Jesus went about healing "every disease and sickness," and now Jesus is giving the disciples authority to heal "every disease and sickness!"

Jesus gave the disciples the power to do everything He did. *"I tell you the truth, anyone who has faith in me will do what I have been doing. He will do even greater things than these, because I am going to the Father"* (John 14:12).

Jesus commanded His followers to, *"Heal the sick, raise the dead, cleanse those who have leprosy, drive out demons"* (Matthew 10:8). This command was never rescinded, it remains in effect today. The church is called to heal the sick.

Did you hear the joke about the Christian dog? He was an amazingly obedient dog. When his masters told him "sit," he would sit down immediately. If they told him to "fetch," the dog would bring them what they were pointing at. Best of all, when they commanded him to "heal," the dog would run to a sick person, lay his paws on his or her head, and begin barking a prayer.

This is a funny story, but it contains a truth which is important to grasp. Properly trained dogs are anxious to please their masters and they are obedient when they are commanded to do a trick. We should behave the same way by being anxious to please our master. Jesus has commanded us to heal so we should heal.

Right before returning to heaven, Jesus said to the disciples, *"Go into all the world and preach the good news to all creation... And these signs will accompany those who believe:...they will place their hands on sick people, and they will get well"* (Mark 16:15-18). We are always excited about what God is going to do, but God is excited about what we are going to do. God is capable of anything; He is just waiting for us to do something.

God is anxiously waiting for one of His children to believe His word. Once our faith lines up with His promise, God gets so excited because finally, He gets to move on our behalf. According to Jesus, *"Everything is possible for him who believes"* (Mark 9:23). You can tap into God's healing power! You can heal the sick!

PRESCRIPTION FOR HEALTH

"Beloved, I wish above all things that
thou mayest prosper and be in health,
even as thy soul prospereth."
(3 John 1:2 KJV)

Dr. Jesus

6,000 Years of Healing History

Top Ten Old Testament Miracle Headlines

1. 90 Year Old Woman Gives Birth
In this astounding story, God fulfilled His promise by healing Sarah's barren womb. Read more in: Genesis 17:17-19; Genesis 21:1-6; Romans 4:19-20; Hebrews 11:11-12

2. Thousands Healed of Deadly Snake Bites
Moses, leader of the Israelites, unveiled a surprise cure when he lifted up a bronze statue of a snake. Whoever looked at the statue was healed from poisonous snake bites. Read more in: Numbers 21:4-9; John 3:14-15

3. Mariam Healed of Leprosy
Moses' sister Mariam was struck with a horrible skin disease. After Moses prayed for her, she was healed. Read more in: Numbers 12:10-15

4. Son of Shunammite Woman Raised from the Dead
Elisha originally healed this woman's barren womb so she could have a child, and when the boy died from a high fever, Elisha raised him from the dead. Read more in: 2 Kings 4:8-37

5. Enemy Army Commander Healed of Leprosy
Naaman was a foreigner, yet he was healed after Elisha told him to dip in the Jordan River seven times. Read more in: 2 Kings 5

6. Dead Man Walking After Touching Elisha's Bones
In this freak miracle, a dead man was thrown into Elisha's tomb. The moment he touched the anointed bones of Elisha, he stood up on his feet. Read more in: 2 Kings 13:20-21

7. Barren Woman Gives Birth
After Hannah cried out to the Lord for healing, she gave birth to a son who she named Samuel. Read more in: 1 Samuel 1

8. Evil King Jeroboam Healed of Withered Hand
The king's hand withered because of his idolatry, but when the prophet prayed for him, his hand returned to normal. Read more in: 1 Kings 13:1-6

9. King Hezekiah Given 15 More Years to Live
He was expected to die, but after the king prayed, Isaiah the prophet told him he would recover. Read more in: 2 King 20:1-11; 2 Chronicles 30-32; Isaiah 38

10. Job Lives 140 Years After God Heals Him
Satan attacked Job with painful sores all over his body. Despite the trouble Job continued to praise God, because of this he was completely healed. Read more in the book of Job.

The Miracle Headlines of Jesus

As a faith building exercise, I encourage you to read about every healing miracle of Jesus.

Jesus drives out an evil spirit in Capernaum	Mark 1:21-28
	Luke 4:36-37
The healing of Simon's mother-in-law	Matthew 8:14-
	15 Mark 1:29-31
	Luke 4:38-39
Healings during the evening time	Matthew 8:16-
	17 Mark 1:32-34
	Luke 4:40-41
The leper	Matthew 8:1-4
	Mark 1:40-44
	Luke 5:12-16
The paralytic	Matthew 9:1-8
	Mark 2:1-12 Luke
	5:17-26
The withered hand	Matthew 12:9-14
	Mark 3:1-6 Luke
	6:6-11
Healings in Galilee	Matthew 12:15-21
	Mark 3:7-12 Luke
	6:17-19
The demonics of Garasene	Matthew 8:28-34
	Mark 5:1-20 Luke
	8:26-39
The rising of Jairus' daughter and the woman with the issue of blood	Matthew 9:18-26
	Mark 5:21-43
	Luke 8:40-56
Healings at Gennesaret	Matthew 14:34-36
	Mark 6:53-56

119

The Syrophoenician (Canaanite) woman	Matthew 15:21-28
	Mark 7:24-30
The deaf-mute	Mark 7:31-37
Blind man at Bethsaida	Mark 8:22-26
The epileptic boy	Matthew 17:14-
	21 Mark 9:14-29
	Luke 9:37-43
Blind Bartimaeus	Matthew 20:29-34
	Mark 10:46-52
	Luke 18:35-43
The centurion's servant	Matthew 8:5-13
	Luke 7:1-10
Healings in the Galilean synagogues	Matthew 4:23
The two blind men	Matthew 9:27-31
The dumb demonic	Matthew 9:32-34
Healings throughout Galilee	Matthew 9:35
The blind and dumb demonic	Matthew 12:22
Healings in the wilderness	Matthew 14:14
Healings on the mountain	Matthew 15:29-31
Healings near the Jordan	Matthew 19:2
Healings in the temple	Matthew 21:14
The widow's son at Nain	Luke 7:11-17
Healings to prove Messiahship to John	Luke 7:21
Healings at Bethsaida	Luke 9:11
The crippled woman who was bent over	Luke 13:10-13
The man with dropsy	Luke 14:1-6
The ear of the high priest's servant	Luke 22:51
Signs in Jerusalem	John 2:23-25
The official's son	John 4:46-54
The lame man at Bethesda	John 5:1-15
The man born blind	John 9:1-34
The raising of Lazarus from the dead	John 11:1-44

Top Ten New Testament Miracle Headlines

1. Crippled Man Causes Uproar in Temple After Being Healed
Two followers of Jesus, Peter and John, healed the crippled man who sat by the temple gate for years. After he was healed, the man went running and leaping and praising God. Read more in: Acts 3:1-10

2. Peter's Shadow Heals the Sick
Peter was so full of God's anointing that even his shadow had the power to heal the sick. Read more in: Acts 5:15

3. Stephen Performs Signs and Wonders
Even though Stephen was only a deacon, his ministry produced miracles which rivaled those of the original apostles. Read more in: Acts 6:8

4. Many Paralytics and Cripples Healed
When Philip traveled to the city of Samaria to preach the gospel, he cast out demons and healed many cripples, producing much joy in the city. Read more in: Acts 8:5-8

5. Simon the Sorcerer Tries to Buy God's Power
Simon was impressed with the miracles of the apostles so he tried to buy the power. To his surprise Peter rebuked him. Read more in: Acts 8:9-25

6. Saul Healed of Blindness
Saul persecuted Christians until he was blinded by a light from heaven while on the road to Damascus. Later his sight was restored when Ananias prayed for him and he became a Christian. Read more in: Acts 9:1-30 and Acts 22

7. Tabitha Raised from the Dead
Peter caused great rejoicing in the church in Joppa when he raised a woman named Tabitha from the dead. Read more in: Acts 9:36-43

8. Slave Girl Set Free
After Paul cast a demon from a fortune-telling slave girl, he and his companion Silas were thrown into prison. But during the night, a surprise earthquake set them free. Read more in: Acts 16:16-40

9. Young Man Who Fell From Second Story Window Raised from the Dead
A boy named Eutychus fell asleep and fell from a second-story window as the apostle Paul was preaching. He hit the ground and was declared dead until Paul prayed for him. Reportedly, after this miraculous raising from the dead, Paul went back to preaching his sermon. Read more in: Acts 20:7-12

10. Snake Fails to Poison Preacher
After a poisonous snake bit Paul, onlookers believed he would die. However, the apostle was unconcerned; he simply shook the snake off his arm. Hours later everyone was surprised to see that he still lived. Because of this, many sick people came to him seeking healing. Read more in: Acts 28:1-10

The Miracles of Church History

Is the age of miracles past? Did miracles cease after the apostolic age? I believe the answer to both these questions is an emphatic "No." God has performed miracles throughout all of church history. God's healing power works in every century, in every generation, and for every person who has the faith to believe for healing.

I believe Jesus is the same yesterday, today, and forever; if Jesus healed when He was on earth, He will heal forever. If it is true that miracles have not ceased, there should be a record of healing testimonies during the last two thousand years. Upon careful examination, it is found that healing power has never been quenched except in the lives of those who stopped believing. Let us look at some healing testimonies through the centuries.

An early church father, **Polycarp** (A.D. 69-155) sat at the feet of John the Apostle and listened to his stories about Jesus. In a letter to the church of Philippi, he exhorts the elders of the church to pray for the sick. Why would he tell them to pray for the sick if healing had ceased?

Clement (A.D. ?-95), a pastor of the church in Rome, wrote detailed instructions for ministers who visit the sick. He said, "Let them, therefore, with fasting and prayer, make their intercessions, and not with the well arranged and fitly ordered words of learning, but as men who have received the gift of healing confidently, to the glory of God."

Justin Martyr (A.D. 100-165) was an influential writer, philosopher, and evangelist during the second century who was eventually beheaded by the Roman government for his beliefs. He emphasized that Christians "have healed and do heal."

Irenaeus (A.D.125-200) wrote a series of books combating false doctrine in the early church. He explained Christians "still heal the sick by laying their hands upon them, and they are made whole. Yea, moreover, as I have said, the dead even have been raised up."

Tertullian (A.D. 160-240) ministered in North Africa. He recounts the healing testimonies of both distinguished men and common people who were cured.

Healing was an important part of the church for the first two hundred years, but then a problem arose. **Origen** (A.D. 185-284) noticed that miracles were becoming less frequent. He mentions the abundance of miracles and supernatural events in the days of the

123

Christ and the early Apostles, then he remarks "but since that time these signs have diminished." Interestingly enough, he pinpoints the reason miracles became infrequent when he says there were no healings because of a lack of holiness among the believers.

When **Constantine** made Christianity the state religion in 313, many joined the church for the sake of political advantages. This changed the focus of Christianity from being a movement which met in homes, to a structured movement that emphasized liturgy and the leadership of bishops. Only sacraments administered by ordained ministers were considered a source of grace. This caused the gifts of the Spirit in ordinary Christians to dry up. As a result, healings and miracles became less frequent in the hands of politically appointed priests and bishops.

Later a new movement arose called monasticism. These were groups of men who became monks in order to devote their lives to prayer. They lived simple, austere lives in order to focus on seeking God. Although some monks decided the amount of suffering one endured was a sign of one's devotion to God, other monks earned a reputation for powerful prayers and miraculous healings.

For example, **Anthony** (A.D. 251-356) who is credited with starting the monastic movement, often prayed for the sick and delivered the demon oppressed. **Athanasius** (A.D. 295-373) writes of one occasion when many sick people gathered outside Anthony's cave seeking prayer. When Anthony came out, "through him the Lord healed the bodily ailments of many present, and cleansed others from evil spirits."

Jerome (A.D. 347-420) writes about another monk, **Hilarion** (A.D. 305-385) who discovered a paralyzed man who was lying near his home. Then, "weeping much and stretching out his hand to the prostrate man he said, 'I bid you in the name of our Lord Jesus Christ, arise and walk.' The words were still on the lips of the speaker when, with miraculous speed, the limbs were strengthened and the man arose and stood firm."

Ambrose (A.D. 340-397), a bishop of Milan, healed a blind man and wrote "as the Father gives the gift of healings, so too does the Son give."

One of the most influential writers and thinkers in Christianity was **Augustine** (A.D. 354-430). In the early years of his ministry, he dismisses the supernatural from church experience. He makes a point "that the witness of the Holy Spirit's presence is no longer given by miracles, but by the love of God in one's

> ## Woman Delivered from Demons
>
> "My name is Yasmeen and I am 26-years-old. For many years I was tormented by demons. They shook my bed in the middle of the night and kept me awake with horrible nightmares.
>
> Eighteen months ago, I saw a poster advertising a Miracle Festival in the Medina suburb of Faisalabad here in Pakistan. The poster announced that Jesus would set people free. I went, hoping to find freedom from the evil spirits that were oppressing me.
>
> On the first and second night of the festival, I tried to listen to the message but the demons kept snatching the ideas and thoughts from my mind. I could feel the demons covering my ears so I would not hear.
>
> But on the third night of the festival, the foreigner who was speaking took authority over every demonic spirit in the Name of Jesus. He commanded them to leave the festival grounds. Suddenly, I could think clearly.
>
> The preacher asked the crowd to pray to Jesus for forgiveness of sin. I cried out to Jesus to save me and immediately I was filled with great peace!
>
> Never again did the demons torment me. After the festival was over, I started attending a local house church that met a short distance from my home. I began to read the Bible and pray every day. I have served Jesus for eighteen months now. I love Him with all of my heart and I am so thankful for everything Jesus has done for me."

heart for the   Church." However, later on in life he changed his mind and wrote about many supernatural events he experienced.

In his classic work, *The City of God*, one chapter is titled "Concerning Miracles Which Were Wrought in Order That the World Might Believe in Christ and Which Cease Not to be Wrought now That the World Does Believe." Augustine says, "For even now, miracles are wrought in the name of Christ." Then, Augustine lists a few of the miracles he has personally experienced including: "healings from blindness, cancer, gout, hemorrhoids, demon possession, and even the raising of the dead."

Unfortunately, Augustine's early opinions concerning the cessation of miracles strongly influenced successive generations of scholars. Even though he wrote about miracles in his later years, his early writings are largely responsible for the belief that miracles ceased.

In spite of the spread of this belief, miracles continued in the lives of many believers. **Benedict** (A.D. 480-547) once prayed for a dead monk who had been crushed by a falling wall at a monastery construction site. The body was laid in his room and Benedict prayed earnestly for an hour. At the end of this time, the monk was raised from the dead and returned to work on the wall.

There are many fantastic stories of healings told about the years A.D. 500-1000. Most of these stories were used to prove the sainthood of worthy individuals. Many sick people traveled to the tombs of saints, or to shrines to seek healing. Churches often collected relics which were said to hold healing power. These relics included the bones of saints, pieces of the true cross, various shrouds, the head of John the Baptist, the tunics of saints, or other holy pieces of history which served as a point of contact for those believing for a miracle.

New leaders arose who started the "traveling friar" movement. These men took vows of poverty, chastity, and obedience. Just like Jesus' disciples, they traveled and preached without taking any extra money or clothing with them. Many miracles were reported in their ministries.

Bernard of Clairvaux (1090-1153) healed the lame, the mute, the blind, and many others who came to him seeking a cure. One boy who had been deaf and mute from birth, began to speak after Bernard prayed for him. The crowds who witnessed the miracle cheered when the saint set the boy up on a bench so he could speak to them.

Hildegard of Bingen (1098-1179) was a woman who flowed in the miraculous. When people came to her for prayer, she used different methods of healing as the Spirit led her. "Sometimes the medium used was a prayer, sometimes a simple word of command, sometimes water which, as in one case, healed paralysis of the tongue." It was said that "scarcely a sick person came to her without being healed."

Francis of Assisi (1181-1226) was an influential force in Christianity who founded the Franciscan order of priests. The preaching of Francis was accompanied with signs and wonders. One time when he was preaching in Narni, he prayed for a man who was completely paralyzed. After Francis made the sign of the cross over his head, the man jumped up and began to walk.

Thomas Aquinas (A.D. 1225-1274) once visited the Vatican. The pope proudly showed the saint all the treasures of the Church: the gold, the silver, the beautiful paintings, and the works of art. The pope turned to Aquinas and proudly said, "No longer can the Church say 'Silver and gold have I none.'" Aquinas sadly looked up and replied, "And no longer can she say, 'Rise up and walk.'" He knew the focus of the church had changed from heavenly power to worldly wealth.

Aquinas was a man of great prayer. He has often been called a genius because of his knowledge, learning, and skill as a writer. Yet he also experienced many miracles in his ministry. One pope declared that Aquinas wrought as many miracles as there are articles in his famous book *Summa Theologica*

Vincent of Farrier (1350-1419) was healed from an illness after seeing a vision of Christ and started his ministry as a result of his personal experience with the healing power of God. When he was preaching in the Netherlands, he prayed for the sick at a set hour each day because there were so many people seeking miracles.

During the Reformation, a new emphasis was placed on the importance of God's Word and on the faith necessary for salvation. The reformers preached a message which emphasized that healing of the soul is more important than healing of the body. But even **Martin Luther** (1483-1546) did occasionally pray for the healing of the sick. One time Luther's good friend, Philip Melancthon, became seriously sick. Luther prayed earnestly for him and confessed all the healing promises from Scripture. Then, he took Melancthon by the hand and said, "Be of good courage, Philip, you shall not die." The man was healed and quickly became healthy again.

John Hus (1373-1415) was a leader of the Moravians who ignited one of the greatest missionary movements in history because of his dedication to prayer. One of the Moravian histories says, "It is...proved, both by facts and by Scripture, that there may always be [gifts of miracles and healings] where there is faith and that they will never be entirely detached from it."

George Fox (1624-91), a Quaker, kept a record of over one hundred miracles. One of the stories from his journal is about the healing of John Banks. The man had terrible pain in his right arm and hand. He sought a cure from doctors but none of them could help. Fox laid his hands on him, and a couple of hours later, the arm was completely restored.

John Wesley (1703-91) who started the Methodist movement was a dynamite preacher who brought salvation to England. Wesley testified to having been healed supernaturally several times. On one occasion, he was stricken with sickness on a Friday and by Sunday, he was barely able to lift his head from the pillow. He relates, "I was obliged to lie down most part of the day, being easy only in that posture. In the evening, beside the pain in my back and head, and the fever which still continued upon me, just as I began to pray I was seized with such a cough that I could hardly speak. At the same time came strongly to my mind, 'These signs shall follow them that believe.' I called on Jesus aloud to increase my faith and to confirm the word of His grace. While I was speaking, my pain vanished away, the fever left me, my bodily strength returned, and for many weeks I felt neither weakness or pain. Unto thee O Lord, do I give thanks."

A powerless church is not what God intended. Jesus gave the original disciples the power to heal and this power has never been taken away from the church. It has been ignored, ridiculed, and doubted; but the power to heal has existed in every generation for those who will believe.

* For more detailed information on the history of healing, I encourage you to read the book by my friend, Dr. Eddie Hyatt, *2,000 Years of Charismatic Christianity*

Words of the Great Healing Evangelists

During the last century there has been an explosion of healing power that is unprecedented in church history. This is a sign of Christ's imminent return. Let us look at what the greatest healing evangelists have said about healing.

"Be not afraid to ask, because God is on the throne waiting to answer your request."
   - **Smith Wigglesworth**

"Disease, like Sin, is God's enemy, and the devil's work, and can never be God's will."
   - John Alexander Dowie

"Beloved, we have not begun to touch the fringes of the knowledge of the power of God."
   - John G. Lake

"Sin and sickness have passed from me to Calvary - salvation and health have passed from Calvary to me."
   - F.F. Bosworth

"Divine healing is wonderful, but divine healing is like the bait that's on the hook. You don't show the fish the hook, you show him the bait. If he gets the bait, he's got the hook, too. If a man can ever be healed and see the power of God...he will then become a believer."
   - William Branham

"God's plan for His saints is more than divine healing. It is divine health."
   - Gordon Lindsey

"Expect a miracle!"
   - Oral Roberts

"People must have proof of the gospel and evidence that Jesus is alive."
   - T.L. Osborn

"I am not a woman of great faith - I am a women with a little faith in the Great God!"
   - Kathryn Kuhlman

Marilyn Hickey's advice to those who want a powerful ministry like hers is, "There are no shortcuts. You must study the Word four or five hours a day and then put even more time into prayer."
- Marilyn Hickey

"That which is considered great today is going to be normal tomorrow!"
- Reinhard Bonnke

"A miracle settles the issue!"
- Mike Francen

"You will no longer be following signs - signs will be following you."
- Benny Hinn

Healing Prayer

Dear Heavenly Father,

I believe you forgive all my sins and heal all my diseases. You wish above all things that I live in health.

Two thousand years ago Jesus died on the cross to pay the price for my sin and to purchase my healing. By the stripes He took on His back, I am healed.

You are the God who heals my diseases. You healed the Israelites in the Old Testament and Jesus healed the sick in the New Testament. Neither one of you change over time. You are the same yesterday, today, and forever. I believe your healing power works today just like it did when Jesus walked the earth.

I renounce the devil's hold on my life. I rebuke every demon of sickness and command Satan to let me be. I am a child of God and no evil can harm me. I repent of every sin, I break every generational curse, and I command sickness to leave my body.

You created me and you can recreate my organs. Your Word says, "Whatsoever you ask for in prayer, believe you have received it, and it shall be yours." I believe you are faithful to keep your word. Lord, I am asking for healing, I believe I am healed, and I receive my healing right now.

In the mighty name of Jesus, Amen.

About the Author

Daniel King and his wife Jessica met in the middle of Africa while they were both on a mission trip. They are in high demand as speakers at churches and conferences all over North America. Their passion, energy, and enthusiasm are enjoyed by audiences everywhere they go.

They are international missionary evangelists who do massive soul-winning festivals in countries around the world. Their passion for the lost has taken them to over fifty nations preaching the gospel to crowds that often exceed 50,000 people.

Daniel was called into the ministry when he was five years old and began to preach when he was six. His parents became missionaries to Mexico when he was ten. When he was fourteen he started a children's ministry that gave him the opportunity to minister in some of America's largest churches while still a teenager.

At the age of fifteen, Daniel read a book where the author encouraged young people to set a goal to earn $1,000,000. Daniel reinterpreted the message and determined to win 1,000,000 people to Christ every year.

Daniel has authored fifteen books including his bestsellers *Healing Power, The Secret of Obed-Edom*, and *Fire Power*. His book *Welcome to the Kingdom* has been given away to tens of thousands of new believers.

THE SECRET OF OBED-EDOM

Unlock the secret to supernatural promotion and a more intimate walk with God. Unleash amazing blessing in your life!

$20.00

MOVE

What is God's will for your life? Learn how to find and fulfill your destiny.

$10.00

POWER OF FASTING

Discover deeper intimacy with God and unleash the answer to your prayers.

$10.00

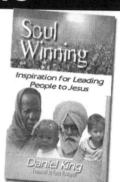

The vision of King Ministries is to lead 1,000,000 people to Jesus every year and to train believers to become leaders.

To contact Daniel & Jessica King:

Write:
King Ministries International
PO Box 701113
Tulsa, OK 74170 USA

King Ministries Canada
PO Box 3401
Morinville, Alberta T8R 1S3 Canada

Call toll-free:
1-877-431-4276

Visit us online:
www.kingministries.com

E-Mail:
daniel@kingministries.com